Kathleen's heart is to see God's people love his Word. Reminding us that the Bible is God's words spoken to his people in the context of the church, she provides very practical tools to equip us to dig deep and mine the treasure of eternal truth. This is the essence of disciple-making and fulfilling Christ's "Great Commission." Every church needs this study.

—**Jane Patete,** Women's Ministries Coordinator,
Presbyterian Church in America

After leading us through masterful studies of several books of the Bible, Kathleen Nielson now gives us an even greater gift: teaching us how she does it! Her literary expertise and love of the Bible that we have seen time and time again are put to their fullest use here, as Dr. Nielson shows us how to view the Bible as both the crucial (and approachable) Word of God and as a literary masterpiece to be immersed in and savored. As do all good teachers, she leads by example, making us excited to dive in and study the Bible by allowing her own excitement to infuse every page. And on a personal note, my wife tells me that Kathleen's material is as trustworthy as it comes. If you want to study the Bible—and, more importantly, know *how* to study it—I can recommend no better teacher than Kathleen Nielson, and no better resource than this book.

—**R. Kent Hughes,** Senior Pastor Emeritus,
College Church in Wheaton

Kathleen Nielson's theological precision, literary background, and deep love for God's Word, combined with the practical tools she provides, will inspire and equip the reader to rightly handle the word of truth. This skillful resource left me with a greater desire to study God's Word.

—**Susan H**unt, ~~Au~~tho~~r, Women's Minis~~try Consultant,
~~~~ ~~an~~d Publications,
~~~~ ~~Chur~~ch in America

Kathleen Nielson has written a substantial but practical guide for those who want to do an effective job of leading Bible studies. All who teach the Bible will profit enormously from this book. She issues the challenge through thoughtful exposition of five basic truths about the Bible, then draws out the practical implications of those truths for actual Bible study. I particularly appreciate the author's emphasis on Bible study leaders learning to master the text for themselves before attempting to teach others. She wants us to know and teach the Bible itself. What a needed emphasis.

—**Stephen Smallman,** CityNet ministries, Philadelphia

I don't know of a greater need among Christians today than better understanding and applying our Bibles. Kathleen Nielson has blessed us with a deeply profound yet thoroughly comprehensible tool to help us do that. I pray that this book will be widely distributed and diligently used by Christians all over the world.

— **Carol Ruvolo,** Bible Teacher, Author of *Turning on the Light: Discovering the Riches of God's Word* and *A Book Like No Other: What's So Special about the Bible*

Kathleen Nielson's book belongs to a very elite circle of books: it covers all the right topics in exactly the right order! As Kathleen pursues the successive topics, a momentum builds up that is akin to the unfolding of the plot line of a novel. The subject of the book has been thoroughly researched, and the personal statements by people who teach the Bible are a welcome touch. The book cannot be better than it is. For people who teach the Bible—or who aspire to teach it—this book will be the gold standard for knowing how to do it right.

—**Leland Ryken,** Professor of English, Wheaton College

Kathleen Nielson, who makes no claim to be a biblical scholar, is a laywoman who has sat at the feet of such scholars and through disciplined study has prepared herself as a master Bible teacher. Nielson gives her readers a fresh and innovative, yet solid and God-glorifying approach, to unlocking the truths of Scripture—not by listening to voices inside themselves in order to make its words justify personal whims and affirm their human choices, but by reading God's words in order to ask what God is saying and how one should respond to him. According to Nielson, you "read [God's Word] with a heart ready to listen and submit." I am delighted to recommend this book, especially to women who are seeking to develop skills in personal Bible study, as a volume for their own personal libraries. This volume will move women toward the goal of unlocking the riches of God's Word and becoming effective in woman-to-woman biblical exposition.

— **Dorothy Patterson,** General Editor of *The Woman's Study Bible,* Professor of Theology in Women's Studies, Southwestern Baptist Theological Seminary

Dissatisfied with leaving Bible study to the professionals while the rest of us are mere recipients of their work, Kathleen Nielson wants all Christians to be involved in thoughtful and faithful Bible study—and tells us how to do it. This is a well-written and wonderfully sane book that deserves the widest circulation.

—**D. A. Carson,** Research Professor of New Testament, Trinity Evangelical Divinity School

Bible Study

Bible Study

Following the Ways of the Word

Kathleen Buswell Nielson

P U B L I S H I N G
P.O. BOX 817 • PHILLIPSBURG • NEW JERSEY 08865-0817

Printed in the United States of America

Library of Congress Cataloging-in-Publication Data

Nielson, Kathleen Buswell.
  Bible study : following the ways of the Word / Kathleen Buswell Nielson.
    p. cm.
  Includes bibliographical references.
  ISBN 978-1-59638-205-3 (pbk.)
  1. Bible–Hermeneutics. I. Title.
  BS476.N54 2011
  220.601–dc22
                                        2010045301

Contents

Preface vii

Introduction ix
What's Happening?

1. If the Bible Is God Speaking . . .   1
   Then How Should We Listen?

2. If the Bible Is Powerful . . .   13
   Then How Should We Approach It?

3. If the Bible Is Understandable . . .   29
   Then How Should We Get It?

4. Asking Questions . . .   43
   A Second Implication

5. If the Bible Is a Literary Work . . .   59
   Then What Should We Expect?

6. From Prose to Poetry . . .   77
   More Literary Explorations

7. If the Bible Is One Whole Story . . .   97
   Then How Should We Read It?

v

CONTENTS

8. Storyline Implications at Work   113

9. So . . .   129
   What Is Bible Study?

10. Looking Ahead . . .   145
    The Challenge

Conclusion   159
Looking Ahead . . . The Promise

Appendix   173
Genre-Specific Study Questions

Notes   179

Preface

THIS BOOK ABOUT BIBLE STUDY is written with a heart full of thanks to all who have led me in the joyful pursuit of studying the Scriptures. First and foremost that includes my husband Niel, who has consistently modeled before me and encouraged in me a passion and a love for God's Word and who is somehow always ready to read (and lovingly critique!) my latest writing, even amid busy work and ministry. What a delight it is to love the Word and love the Lord together.

Thanks are due to many others, including parents and family, pastors and teachers, and countless cohorts in the activity of Bible study. Many friends in ministry have graciously sent comments sharing their wisdom and experience. I am grateful for these rich words and privileged to include them in text boxes throughout the chapters, all with the permission of the writers. Most of the quoted voices come from people I have observed "in action" and served with in ministry. How encouraging it is to be part of a chorus of voices passionately concerned about this topic! The *whole* chorus is huge and global; any one of us knows only a portion, only a hint. A small percentage of the voices quoted here comes from outside the

United States. Those voices bring valued perspective, challenge, and clarification of the universal issues at stake.

The smaller portion of the quoted material comes from men; the vast majority was sent by women who are leaders in ministry across the country and the world. The women acknowledged serve in the areas of Christian education and women's Bible study. Clearly, my context of ministry has led me to connect most deeply with other women, and I am grateful for these connections. This book emerges out of my own study and experience, but not with any attempt to shape the content specifically for women; the book is about Bible study, not women's ministry in particular. Some have observed that women in general do a better job of answering the call for serious Bible study than men do. I offer no conclusions on this matter—only prayers that God will raise up in his church huge, loving armies of both men and women who are well armed with the sword of the Spirit, which is the Word of God.

Introduction

What's Happening?

Thoughts on Bible study, with
three perceptions concerning:

1. The Church
2. Authority
3. Words

BIBLE STUDY . . . EVERYBODY'S DOING IT. In churches and
dorms and neighborhoods all across the nation and the world,
groups of people are drawn together for the stated purpose
of studying the most influential book in human history. The
Word of God is invading the world. This book celebrates Bible
study, and at the same time it asks the question: Just what *is*
Bible study? Is it possible to pinpoint a cluster—even a flexible cluster—of characteristics that must be present for "Bible
study" to be identifiable and effective? Where should we begin
in order to answer that question?

These questions and this book arise from the observation that the generally accepted cluster of characteristics necessary for Bible study is expanding rapidly. Such expansion has a wonderfully positive side, as the Word of God evidences its ability to speak in all kinds of ways and contexts. And yet it is helpful for Christians—the ones who claim to believe the Bible—to stop and think it through, to see what's happening around us, and most of all to examine our course in light of the Bible itself.

Such examination should happen from all sorts of perspectives; I want to acknowledge that mine is one of many within the Christian family. Mine is not the perspective of a biblical scholar trained in Greek and Hebrew—crucial as that perspective is. Rather, mine is the perspective of a layperson who has benefited from such scholars, who has been lovingly trained in biblically based churches, and who has participated in, led, written materials for, and spoken to Bible study groups for a few decades—mainly women's groups. I should add that I am an American, a female, a middle-aged person, and a teacher formally educated in literary studies. Each of these categories provides both a limitation and an advantage in perspective. I believe it is people like me—not professional biblical scholars, but laypeople of all stripes—who at this point in time need to think through exactly what we are doing in Bible study.

The scholars and pastors are there doing the heavy work, but we cannot leave the work to them. Most Bible study groups do not enjoy the privilege of being led regularly by Greek or Hebrew professors, or even by pastors. Some groups benefit from the oversight of trained leaders, and indeed, the challenge ahead is to train more and more. Currently, many untrained laypeople, even in churches with strong pastors who preach and teach the Word, find themselves members or even leaders of a "Bible study" without having had the opportunity to consider carefully just what that term might mean.

Living out both the limitations and the advantages of my perspective, I've observed three perceptions at work in and around the church, perceptions that both clarify and complicate the task of getting down to the basics of Bible study. The first is a perception concerning the *church*. This perception is that the church, both on the local level and in the larger sense, consists of two classes: the professionals (who do the serious study of the Scriptures) and the rest (who simply benefit from the writing and teaching of the professionals). I wonder if we are giving up some of the benefits dearly paid for by the Reformers, who gave their labor and their lives to translate the Scriptures and make them available to all. Now, it seems, we would too easily hand them back to a group of experts to digest and interpret them for us. Many Bible study groups have no interest in spending a lot of energy digging into a text of Scripture; they are busy, this is not their expertise, and it's frankly much easier to discuss a short chapter of a Christian book or watch a video together. Such activities can be good, especially if they do not substitute for Bible study.

In a speech to Beeson Divinity School seminary students, one of those experts named John Piper told those students to stop reading so much John Piper and start reading the Bible. His example was Luther, who gave himself to biblical study as primary, "elevated above" the reading of theologians and church fathers. "I know from experience," Piper said, "and I know from observation pastors do not study their Bibles. They read Piper and other such books, which is a colossal mistake. Read and study your Bibles. You don't know your Bibles yet. Could you give an exposition of Ezekiel? Could you give an exposition of Ecclesiastes?"[1] Even the experts-in-training are looking to experts rather than to the Scriptures themselves!

The very best experts—including Piper—know that they are not the ones to look to ultimately, but that the Bible itself is the only sufficient final authority for every person. The best experts are those who not only study hard to share the fruit of their labor, but also want to train others to read and study the Scriptures themselves, so that they can then train others to read and study the Scriptures themselves . . . and on and on.

To be clear, my aim in this book is not to speak as an expert in biblical matters. English is my field, and that will come through! My aim is to take the treasures learned under the authority of pastors especially, as well as all kinds of scholars, and to discuss how we laypeople can connect such treasures to the study of the Bible. We will discuss this further.

The second perception concerns *authority* and might seem to challenge the first one. This perception, which exists in the general culture (especially the general American culture) and has seeped into the church, is that no one has the right to act as an authority over me. We are all familiar with the cases of children suing parents, or of young people desiring from adults vulnerability and affirmation more than wisdom and knowledge. Ultimately, of course, the instinct to reject authority reflects the rebellion of fallen humankind against a sovereign Lord God. Such rebellion has existed since Adam, but it shows itself openly in cultures that are turning away from even outward submission to the Word of God.

A Word from God implies a word from outside us, a breaking into our lives by some transcendent being to whom we are obliged to listen. But our culture is listening much more closely to voices inside ourselves; we tend to read words and say how they make us feel, rather than read words and ask what they say and how we should rightly respond. To read the Bible as the authoritative Word of God means to read it with a heart ready to listen and submit. This is a radical activity in a culture that does not embrace the legitimacy of authority.

How does this perception concerning authority fit with the perception concerning the church? Wouldn't the perception of a group of professionals imply a kind of authority on their part—against which the rest of the church might struggle? In fact, biblical scholars are often not perceived to be those with an authoritative voice, but rather those who chose that specialty and who can be of huge help and comfort to the rest of us as needed. They are simply part of the whole ongoing conversation, with all kinds of interesting insights as they interact with the words of Scripture in new and creative ways. Perhaps part of the reason many are happy to leave the work of Bible study to the specialists is that such work is not generally perceived to be authoritative work—that is, work that deals with an authoritative Word. Perhaps if laypeople more deeply respected the authority of the Word, there might exist a more passionate and widespread interest in being led and trained by those who have studied it deeply.

Even contemporary newscasting reveals our distaste for authority. The public doesn't seem to want newscasters who simply impart facts as objectively as possible. Rather, people want news shows and talk shows that allow them to interact and hear other people's views and share theirs, whether via Twitter or online polls or chat rooms. News these days might be defined as the sum of what everybody thinks. The news, then, is not something outside myself that I learn; rather, it is my interaction with others as we all together process ongoing stories of the day. It is easy to make the jump to seeing Bible study as simply a group processing of words, a Twittering sort of interaction, with the point being not what the authoritative Word speaks, but rather the sum of what everybody thinks. We will discuss this further.

The third perception, again existing generally and bleeding into the church, concerns *words*. It is that words lack the power to communicate truth. I do not have time or proper expertise to explore all the intricacies of postmodern and post-postmodern language theory, but a few observations are in order as we begin to consider what it means to study a book of words given to us by God. To my remark that we are no longer a culture that respects words, a friend responded, "What do you mean? More of us spend more time dealing with words than have people at any other time in history!" This is true. With the advent of the Internet and all the associated and growing technology, we traffic in words more routinely than ever before. We can access or delete thousands and millions of words with the touch of a button.

The point, however, is not the amount or the accessibility of words, but rather our view of words. We traffic in them easily, but we do not generally trust them to carry a weight of meaning across that bridge that stretches from a speaker or author, on one side, to the one who hears or reads, on the other. We don't mind this; in fact, we celebrate the dance of words across the bridge and the imaginative reassembling of them by the receiver on the other side. This wonderful dance has always occurred, of course, as words must enter the consciousness of receivers who have unique sets of understandings and experiences for processing them. I can send across the bridge the words *home* and *father*, confident that these words arouse different thoughts and pictures within each person who receives them. Yet cannot we also be confident of a quite basic and universally understood meaning to these words, a core meaning intended by the giver and understandable by the receiver?

To put the question another way, should we follow skippingly where Humpty Dumpty tries to lead Alice, in *Through the Looking Glass?* In the course of their discussion of birthdays and presents, Humpty Dumpty cries:

> "There's glory for you!"
>
> "I don't know what you mean by 'glory,'" Alice said.
>
> Humpty Dumpty smiled contemptuously. "Of course you don't—till I tell you. I meant 'there's a nice knock-down argument for you!'"
>
> "But 'glory' doesn't mean 'a nice knock-down argument,'" Alice objected.
>
> "When *I* use a word," Humpty Dumpty said in rather a scornful tone, "it means just what I choose it to mean—neither more nor less."
>
> "The question is," said Alice, "whether you *can* make words mean so many different things."
>
> "The question is," said Humpty Dumpty, "which is to be master—that's all."[2]

No question that Humpty Dumpty (and Lewis Carroll!) makes the words dance! But Alice's concern is ours here: whether or not both the giver and the receiver of the words can assume a core of commonly understood meaning to them, and trust them to dance across that bridge of understanding without totally changing shape in the process. How far should we go in questioning the meaning of the word *is?*

Kevin Vanhoozer explores with expertise the intricacies of language and hermeneutical theory in his book *Is There a Meaning in This Text? The Bible, the Reader, and the Morality of Literary Knowledge.* He leads his reader in learning humility from theorists who challenge an overconfident assertion of exact meaning. But he also powerfully challenges those theorists who deny the possibility of receiving meaning intended by an author—those theorists who have in fact proclaimed the death of the author in the literary process. Vanhoozer bases his argument in a biblical understanding of God, God's Trinitarian nature, and God as the source of all meaningful communication. It is no mistake, says Vanhoozer, that talk of the death of the author has come along with talk of the death of God.[3]

A more recent book, Vern Poythress's *In the Beginning Was the Word*, beautifully develops a whole theology of language grounded in a biblical view of the triune God as the source of all words and meaning.[4] Poythress reminds us that words, any words, have meaning only in relation to the God who exists and who spoke the universe into being by his Son, with the breath of the Spirit. Human beings use words meaningfully because they image God their Creator, whether they acknowledge this or not.

Indeed, it makes all the difference in the world whether we view the universe as a dance of random particles or as a direct creation of God who spoke it into being and preserves it by his word for the end he ordains. The apostle Peter rebukes those who doubt God's coming judgment by reminding them that God's sure word encompasses the whole scope of human history:

> For they deliberately overlook this fact, that the heavens existed long ago, and the earth was formed out of water and through water by the word of God, and that by means of these the world that then existed was deluged with water and perished. But by the same word the heavens and earth that now exist are stored up for fire, being kept until the day of judgment and destruction of the ungodly. (2 Peter 3:5–7)

The implications of all this for Bible study are huge. If we study with the assumption that we as readers use our individual contexts and experiences to shape our own meanings from the words, then Bible study will consist mainly of a series of personal reactions and opinions. The dance will be chaotic and, in the end, narcissistic. On the other hand, if we study with the assumption that God intends to give us meaning that we can receive more or less clearly through words, then Bible study will consist of learning to "dig into" the words as carefully as possible, so that we come closer and closer to the meaning God intends us to receive. We will come closer to *him*, for the words come from him. That's the point. We will grow to love the divine master director of this dance, which is as beautiful as the universe he created.

I would venture to guess that most "Bible studiers" would claim to operate under the latter assumption but have imbibed and come to enjoy the taste of the former. The implications grow even huger when we unpack the special nature of Scripture's inspired words. We will discuss this further.

Clearly, these three perceptions are all intertwined, with the word issues at the heart of them. These perceptions will be intertwined with the discussion that follows in this book—with the word issues at the heart of it. It is God's Word that teaches us how the church, the body of Christ, must be fully equipped for the mission of making disciples in these last days. That equipping happens through the Word. It is God's Word that teaches his authoritative and loving rule, through his commands that must be obeyed. It is God's Word that is living and active, sharper than any two-edged sword (Heb. 4:12).

What huge claims for itself the Word makes! Do we believe them and operate according to them? These claims should be our starting point for any Bible study, and to these claims we will now give attention. Having sensed the overall complexity of the subject and the need to clarify this crucial activity of Bible study, we will focus in the following chapters on five key truths about what the Bible is. Knowing what it is will help us learn how to study it. Each truth, then, will lead to specific implications for Bible study.

1

If the Bible Is God Speaking . . .

Then How Should We Listen?

Truth №1: The Bible is God speaking.

Implications for study:

1. The nature of Bible study
2. The goal of Bible study
3. Our attitude in study

IT'S THE WORLD'S NUMBER-ONE BEST-SELLING BOOK. It's been translated into well over 2,000 languages, and that number is increasing all the time. It's the foundational text of Western civilization. Many Americans have dozens of copies in their homes. Yet in spite of the dramatic proliferation of this book and in spite of all the books written by all the experts about this

1

book, we may be in general less acquainted with its contents than many in the centuries preceding us. What is this book?

Perhaps the most basic element in the cluster of characteristics essential for Bible study is a clear understanding and communication of what Scripture is. What are we studying? The truths about Scripture in these next chapters appear increasingly radical in the world in which we live. New participants in Bible studies often include those who have only the vaguest sense of the nature of this book. Actually, we should hope that is true, in the sense that we hope our churches and our Bible studies will attract many who do not yet know either the Scriptures or the Lord of the Scriptures.

A new generation is emerging, one not steeped in the old Bible stories most people used to know. British author Vaughan Roberts tells an amazing story of a visiting instructor in a primary school who asked the children to name the person who knocked down the wall of Jericho. Nervous silence ensued, broken by one child's response: "Please sir, my name is Bruce Jones. I don't know who did it but it wasn't me."[1] The incident (admittedly unverified!) progresses through several more layers of ignorance, culminating in a letter from the Department of Education regretting the reported damage to the walls of Jericho and offering to cover the cost upon receiving an estimate.

In the midst of growing oblivion, the truths of just what the Bible is stand out as exceedingly precious, to be cherished and mused on and enthusiastically communicated. Not every Bible study should begin with a treatise on the nature of Scripture. However, if these truths are true, then the light of their truth must emerge, in one way or another, as the Bible is studied. Standing on these truths offers us a clear perspective on the Bible and what it means to study it. Let's begin with perhaps the most basic truth: the Bible is God speaking.

"Many people consider the Bible inspiring but not inspired . . . a book to be respected, but not read . . . a book for the clergy but not the laity . . . a book for good, religious people but not for sinners. For many, its religious stories are irrelevant to everyday people in everyday life. We must teach that God speaks through the Bible, and that he speaks into our everyday lives, with truth and power to change us."

—Debbie Seward, Bible study leader,
College Church in Wheaton, Illinois

The Bible Is God Speaking

In his helpful basic introduction to the Scriptures, *I Believe in the Bible*, David Jackman makes it clear right at the start: "The Bible is not a book about God; it is God speaking to us."[2] I love this starting point, one that straightens out right away a whole host of common misconceptions, such as that the Bible is a set of propositions to be learned, or that the Bible is an old dead book we have to keep resurrecting for new times and places. Such misconceptions separate the words on the page from the speaker whose breath breathed them to his creation.

I love this starting point also because Jackman dares to say simply what theologians are continually debating in complex detail. We need professional scholars and theologians, and we must learn from them. We should look into a classic like Carl Henry's *God, Revelation, and Authority*.[3] We should read the Chicago Statement on Biblical Inerrancy, which is included in volume 4 of Henry's work. We should study the doctrines of the inspiration and inerrancy of Scripture and search Scripture for its truths in these matters. If the Bible is actually anything like what it claims, then it deserves careful attention—as careful as we are capable of. Such care will enable laypeople to glean and communicate these truths in a simple but not simplistic way that makes sense to many fellow studiers of the Bible.

We begin, then, with the simple but huge truth of God speaking. In Scripture itself God appears as a word-speaker from the very beginning, from the moment he said, "Let there be light," and there was light. Psalm 33:6 puts it this way:

> By the word of the LORD the heavens were made,
>   and by the breath of his mouth all their host.

As the Bible consistently celebrates this powerful creative word, we begin to sense that God's word appears not as a disconnected thing that logically causes something else to happen; rather, in the very breath of his word being uttered, the creation happens! When we learn that the Hebrew word for *breath* (*ruach*) is also the word for *spirit* (as in the *Spirit of God* in Gen. 1:2), and when we go on to learn, for example in Colossians 1:16, that by Jesus Christ the Son all things were created, we begin to grasp the working of the triune God through his word from the beginning.

God pours out his three-personed self through his word. When we land in John 1 and read about the Word who in the beginning was with God, and was God, and through whom all things were made, we see even more deeply into the personal meaning of God's word—even to the point of its being made flesh to dwell among us. God's being a word-speaker is the most personal extension of his very self into his creation.

All this helps clarify "the inspiration of Scripture," a crucial doctrinal tenet. In the context of Bible study groups, it is helpful to see this tenet in the most personal sense, as we understand that the Creator God personally "breathed out" all Scripture, according to Paul in 2 Timothy 3:16. The process of God's breathing it out is never explained in a technical way, but it is unfolded by Peter, who describes the writers of Scripture as men who "spoke from God as they were carried along by the Holy Spirit" (2 Peter 1:21).

I'll never forget a certain training session for various teaching leaders at College Church in Wheaton. The young pastor leading the session spent considerable time talking about these writers' being "carried along" by the Spirit as they wrote down the words of Scripture. I knew this basic doctrine, and I remember thinking that this instruction would be helpful for newer leaders. My pastor, however, proceeded to talk about how Luke used the same word we translate "carried along" to describe Paul's ship, which in Acts 27:13–17 was "driven along" by a tempestuous wind, a northeaster so strong that they simply had to give way to it. He vividly described that wind filling up the sails of Paul's boat and driving it along the coast of Crete. Then he asked us to keep that picture in mind as we considered the powerful wind of the Spirit that *carried along* these writers.

These writers did "speak"; they did indeed actively author the words. And yet they authored them as their hearts and minds were filled, blown full, driven along by the wind of the Holy Spirit's breath, God's breath, so that every word they wrote was exactly the one the divine Author intended to speak to us. This is why we can say that Scripture is inerrant in the original manuscripts—because the perfect, sovereign God breathed it out and carried those writers along. That day, in that class at church, I began not just to understand better this doctrine of inspiration but to love it more—to love more the God who would so powerfully and perfectly speak himself to us in words. This was crucial training for Bible study.

How amazing that God has not turned away and withdrawn his word to a human race that has been made up of rebels against that word since Adam and Eve disobeyed his command in the garden of Eden. But God did not stop speaking. He came to Adam and Eve and spoke a promise—a promise that one day the seed of the woman would bruise the head of the evil serpent who introduced sin into the world. The entire remainder of the Bible reveals the working out of that promise, ultimately fulfilled in the Word made flesh, Jesus Christ the Son of God. God overflows with words for us. He doesn't hide; he reveals himself and pours himself out through his word as he speaks to us, by his Spirit, ultimately through Christ.

"Some have told me that the Bible is outdated and can't meet all our needs in today's world. I deal with these kinds of issues by focusing in on what the Bible says about itself, and emphasizing that if it is in error about what it says about itself, then it can't be trusted to speak in any area because it isn't the Word of God. But if it is the Word of God, we must submit ourselves to all of it, not just the parts we like."

—Carol Ruvolo, author, Bible study leader, Heritage Christian Fellowship, Albuquerque, New Mexico

---

Implications

The Nature of Bible Study

Three important implications arise from this foundational truth about the inspiration of Scripture. The first implication concerns the nature of Bible study: it is personal. Bible study is not primarily a matter of learning propositions or getting facts straight; it is a matter of hearing God speak to us. I am not saying that Bible study does not involve rigorous work and much learning. It does, as we will discuss. But the point is that the work and learning happen in relationship—first with the Lord God to whom we're listening, and also with those around us who are related to us (or perhaps being drawn into relationship with us) through him, as we listen to his words together.

Many Bible studies these days emphasize this aspect of personal relationship, but too often the relational elements are separated from the elements of textual study, with the assumption that it is more sensitive and fulfilling to talk, pray, and encourage each other than to engage in intellectual analysis of words on a page. Such a false dichotomy thrusts aside a love letter from the one being whose words can pierce and fully satisfy a soul needy for loving relationship. Indeed, the context of loving interaction with others is beautiful and essential. But how amazing, in that context, to be privileged to hear from the Lord our Maker. How far away from sterile intellectual analysis is the process of deeply studying God's Word. As we lean together over a biblical text to study it, we are in effect leaning in closer to the breath of God.

We were made to receive God's words. And we were made to receive them not just individually but together, as his people. Taking in God's words is not simply a mental exercise that we

7

then have to make personal; it is itself a relational activity—
based on the primary relationship with the God who is there
and who speaks to us. Perhaps sometimes we just don't believe
he's there, and we're left to acknowledge only ourselves.

In a Bible study group, the actual study of the Bible is the
foundation of the personal, relational aspect of the gathering.
In a Bible study we come together to take in the words of our
God who is there and who made us, loves us, and speaks to
us—and who binds us together in a unity of the Spirit, which
is stronger than the ties we can create ourselves.

The Goal of Bible Study

If the first implication of the fact that the Bible is God
speaking concerns the nature of Bible study, the second implication concerns its goal—for people to know God through
listening to him speak. This makes logical sense: if a Bible
study is personal at its core, then the primary goal must be
for each person and all the people together to develop this
personal relationship with God and through him with each
other. This goal must encompass both unbelievers' coming
to know God initially as well as believers' coming to know
God better. When Jesus prayed for his disciples just before his
death, he prayed for all those who would believe in him, that
they might be one in him "so that the world may believe that
you have sent me" (John 17:20–23).

The goal for the time between Jesus' first coming and his
second coming is for the world to come to know him as his
disciples reproduce themselves. The Great Commission in
Matthew 28 is received by Jesus' first disciples and then, by its
very nature, passed on to every subsequent follower of Jesus,
so that the process of new disciples' being baptized and taught

should continue to expand even to the end of this age when Jesus will come again. The first disciples participated in the crucial work of completing God's inspired Word, as the promised Holy Spirit brought the truth of Jesus' life and teaching perfectly to their minds, filling their sails as they wrote down the New Testament books. We later followers of Christ continue to press on with God's Word as our primary tool. The activity of Bible study must be seen in the context of this goal: that the world would come to know God through his Son.

"I've never experienced anyone who did not open the Bible without respect. They seem to perceive it as being God's book. However, the Bible is often a totally unknown book to a person attending a Bible study for the first time. It may only be a 'table book,' or this person may not even own a Bible. It's important to offer a Bible to anyone who wants one. In the first small-group session, I never assume that everyone knows how to find a biblical text reference."

—Nancy Hawley, Bible study teacher,
College Church in Wheaton, Illinois

Has the focus of many Bible studies become ingrown? How often do we Christians actually view ourselves as being in training to make other disciples, even through our Bible study? One wonderful way to expand our focus is to participate in a Bible study that includes nonbelievers or new believers or to change our current studies by including new people, perhaps even our own friends and neighbors.

People new to the Scriptures ask questions that longtime believers would never ask and lead a group to notice things about what God says that those of us in our established ruts might never notice. To witness someone else hearing God speak personally to him or her for the first time strengthens our own faith in God's Word and the personal God who speaks it. From the perspective of one being drawn to faith, it is powerful and compelling to witness believers in the act of loving God and loving to hear his Word. In the end, taking to heart this large goal of seeing the world around us come to know God is a step of obedience to the Word itself, and that obedience brings both joy to us and ultimately glory to God. Bible studies do feed Christians, but that feeding is part of a larger picture, of a world full of disciples being fed to feed others.

"I just heard this story from a woman who leads a small group. . . . One member of her group has not yet committed her life to Christ, but she keeps coming to the study and participating in the small group. She loves the relationships of love, clearly. Last week, after one Sunday of attending church with this small-group leader, the young woman had the courage to go to church on her own. She's growing in the graces, being showered with God's love and Word on a regular basis."

—Kari Stainback, Director of Women's Ministries, Park Cities Presbyterian Church, Dallas, Texas

---

I have seen this goal in action, along with the joy it brings, most often in churches where the leaders have established a vision for the world, and often in places in the world where gospel outreach is growing in spite of governments that do not approve. In some such countries, for example, where international Christian churches are allowed to meet, people from all over the world gather, drawn to these churches by their vibrant fellowship, their strong preaching, and often their welcoming Bible study groups. Many people receive the gospel and carry it back to their various places of origin. There is an excitement to see new converts—an excitement that inevitably spills into the immediate community, whether it's allowed to do so or not.

Our Attitude during Study

The third implication concerns the attitude with which we approach Bible study. We need an attitude of humility. If the Bible is God speaking, then we should not be too quick to speak ourselves, before we have listened well to him. Humpty Dumpty got it right: the question is which is to be master. If there is a God and he speaks, then his word is authoritative, a master's word, calling for reverence and submission. If there is a God and he speaks, then we will be full of prayer and supplication for his help as we take in his Word. "Your hands have made and fashioned me," humbly prays the psalmist; "give me understanding that I may learn your commandments" (Ps. 119:73).

We have to keep acknowledging the fact that each person brings unique contexts and experiences to Scripture's words, all of which will affect the process of understanding them. An attitude of humility will lead us to examine rather than simply acknowledge this state of affairs. After such acknowledgment, should we not go on to ask how we can keep our contexts and experiences from turning into hard interpretive grids? How can we more and more fully open ourselves, each with our marvelous uniqueness, to become those in whom the Word can dwell richly? How can we learn to receive these words in ways that will please the God who spoke them? We will discuss various approaches and questions that can help. But perhaps most fundamental is the attitude of our hearts—humility that fears God and knows the weight of his Word.

Connecting the words of Scripture to the God who speaks them with his very breath restores in us that attitude toward the Word found in the Word: one of fear and trembling. It's also an attitude of delight and joy and wonder, as we will discuss, but it's consistently an attitude of humble fear. After rehearsing the works of God proclaimed in his Word, the prophet Habakkuk stops and says:

> I hear, and my body trembles;
>   my lips quiver at the sound;
> rottenness enters into my bones;
>   my legs tremble beneath me. (Hab. 3:16)

The apostle Peter, even as he wrote inspired words explaining the inspiration of Scripture, took on a solemn tone as he affirmed the surety of the prophetic word, "to which you will do well to pay attention as to a lamp shining in a dark place, until the day dawns and the morning star rises in your hearts" (2 Peter 1:19). That beautiful admonishment should rouse in us not only wonder that God should speak through his Word, but also a humble fear that compels us to pay attention and listen prayerfully.

To start with the truth that the Bible is God speaking gives us the most important perspective when we gather to study the Bible. The next truth encourages us as we begin to handle the words.

2

If the Bible Is Powerful . . .

Then How Should We Approach It?

Truth №2: The Bible is powerful.

Implications for study:

1. Respect for the words: observation and translation
2. Sufficiency of the words

The Bible Is Powerful

The second truth follows the first: if Scripture is breathed out by the God who by the breath of his mouth created the heavens, then Scripture must indeed be powerful. Scripture makes dramatic claims about what it is and what it can do. Immediately before Paul's teaching about Scripture's being God-breathed, his initial comment about these "sacred writings" is that they "are able to make you wise for salvation through faith in Christ Jesus" (2 Tim. 3:15). Before moving on, we should stop and take note of this foundational claim that the Bible leads people to understand and receive salvation in Christ.

"The Scriptures are powerful to save. In Eastern Turkey we met a man who had been a Christian—the only Christian in his city of 75,000—for about five years. Ugur had become dissatisfied with Islam and wanted to know the truth about God. So he went to Istanbul for university and studied all the holy books he could find. He investigated Hinduism, Buddhism, and other world religions but couldn't find the truth. Then a friend suggested the holy book of the Christians. Ugur ordered a Bible from a Web site. He told us that, as he began reading the Gospels in his quest for truth, Truth jumped off the page. This Truth was a person, the person of Jesus Christ. The Bible is that powerful. It can take a person from darkness to light. Ugur gave up everything in his pursuit of Christ. He was mocked and threatened and cut off from his family. Ultimately, he was stabbed to death at a Bible distribution center just three years after we were privileged to meet him."

—Keri Folmar, pastor's wife and Bible study teacher, United Christian Church of Dubai, United Arab Emirates

The previous chapter established as the goal for Bible study that the world would come to know this God who speaks.

We come to know him through his salvation offered in Christ and revealed throughout the Scriptures. How ironic it would be to study the Bible and yet ignore Scripture's foundational power to make people wise for salvation, from its beginning point to its end point, when we will shine perfectly with Christ's own holiness. Wisdom for salvation comes first—followed by Scripture's power to speak into every ensuing stage of gospel growth and discipleship. These words from God are "profitable for teaching, for reproof, for correction, and for training in righteousness, that the man of God may be competent, equipped for every good work" (2 Tim. 3:16–17).

How does this happen? How does this comprehensive power take effect? Lest we answer that question too quickly, R. C. Sproul offers a valuable warning, as he writes of his frustration at being asked to speak and "make the Bible come alive!"

> I had to force myself to swallow my words. I wanted to say, "You want me to make the Bible come alive? I didn't know that it had died. In fact, I never even heard that it was ill. Who was the attending physician at the Bible's demise?" No, I can't make the Bible come alive for anyone. The Bible is already alive. It makes me come alive.[1]

Other great works we do need to bring to life. Even in teaching what the world would call "inspired" literature like Shakespeare or Dante, I have had to work hard to make the words come to life for certain skeptical college students.

But Scripture is different from any other writing. It takes work to "get into it," yes. But it is living and active with the breath of God. According to Hebrews, "the word of God is living and active, sharper than any two-edged sword, piercing to the division of soul and of spirit, of joints and of marrow, and discerning the thoughts and intentions of the heart" (Heb. 4:12). The life and activity pictured here move through flesh into inner spiritual regions we cannot see with our physical eyes. The double-edged sword penetrates invisible realities. Only by faith do we know that those realities truly exist; we peer into them, seeing as in a mirror dimly. This sword's work is supernatural and happens by the power of the Spirit who inspired the words in the first place. This much makes sense: if the physical universe sprang into being at God's word, why should not conviction and transformation and new life spring up in hearts at his word? His word is that alive and active and powerful not on its own, but because he speaks it.

The Word itself tells us of its living power, and history confirms it. What would have impelled those ancient copiers of the early manuscripts to take such remarkable care—the kind of care evidenced by the discovery of the Dead Sea Scrolls in 1947? These manuscripts, almost two thousand years old, corroborated the accuracy of the manuscripts from the Middle Ages, which had until then been the oldest known. What would have caused martyrs to die for possessing the Scriptures, or for daring, like William Tyndale, to translate it for others? Why have so many leaders, from ancient Roman emperors to more contemporary dictators, worked so vehemently to stamp it out?

If God's Word were not so potent, it would not be so feared, in all sorts of good and bad ways. God has supernaturally watched over his Word, sending it forth to accomplish his saving purposes, which will not fail. The last word about the power of the Word is God's:

> For as the rain and the snow come down from heaven
>   and do not return there but water the earth,

making it bring forth and sprout,
  giving seed to the sower and bread to the eater,
so shall my word be that goes out from my mouth;
  it shall not return to me empty,
but it shall accomplish that which I purpose,
  and shall succeed in the thing for which I sent it.
    (Isa. 55:10–11)

Implications

Respect for the Words

What implications for Bible study grow from this truth of the power of God's Word? The first is that we should study with respect for the words. This implication becomes complicated in the midst of a culture that likes (Humpty Dumpty style) to create or re-create the meanings of words more than to respect the meanings of words. However, if it is true that God's Spirit inspired the writers of Scripture to write down exactly the words God intended, and if those words are described in Scripture as living and active and powerful to accomplish what God intends, then does it not follow that we should begin the process of Bible study by giving the most careful attention to the words? The most helpful and practical first step in a Bible study is to *observe the words.*

Before discussing this process of observation, however, we must acknowledge the knotty issue of *translation.* If observing the words is key, then exactly which words we're observing will be key. We're not observing concepts or general ideas; we're observing words. Many current theorists tend to speak of words simply as conveyers of meaning, separating the particular words from the meaning intended by the author. The result is that the actual words become less important than the meaning; if we can determine the meaning intended, we can put that meaning into other words for new people and places and times.

All translations put meaning into other words. That is the nature of the process. However, various translations emphasize more or less an acknowledged core meaning of the original words. For example, a translation that gives greater emphasis to maintaining the acknowledged core meaning would translate Matthew 9:10: "And as Jesus reclined at table in the house" (ESV). A translation that is less "literal" (not as close to the acknowledged core meaning of the original words) takes into account the cultural information that reclining at someone else's house in ancient times meant that one was there for dinner. Today's New International Version (TNIV) translates the perceived meaning of that same verse: "While Jesus was having dinner at Matthew's house." Both are translations of meaning from the original words to the new ones. Both make some changes, because neither Jesus' name nor "at table" appears in the Greek, which reads most literally "while he was reclining in the house."[2] But the willingness of the TNIV to change the original words more extensively for the sake of contextual meaning puts it closer to what is called "dynamic equivalency" than to "essentially literal" translation. Clearly, no readable translation is purely literal. When I'm aiming for "purely literal," I go to an interlinear translation, which is hugely helpful in studying but would be wooden and ridiculous to try to read as my primary text in English.

In an ideal world, we would all be able to read the words in the original Hebrew and Greek. Certainly we should all find both written helps and live people who can explain the Hebrew and Greek words to us, as we study more and more in depth. I would not want to study a passage without my *Vine's Complete*

Expository Dictionary of Old and New Testament Words.[3] We should all eventually be learning about these ancient languages, as we're increasingly drawn into careful study of the biblical texts. But for us laypeople who don't have the languages, how should we choose a translation for our study?

When I'm working with a Bible study group, I do not insist on a particular translation. However, I am always ready to recommend a translation and to explain why I believe it offers me best access to the words God originally inspired to be written down. This is the crux of my standard of judgment: I want to use a translation that gets me as close as possible to the words God by his Spirit led the original writers to write. Granted, those words benefit from cultural and contextual explanation. I do not believe that is the main job of the translator. Here is one situation where the specialists have perhaps not considered carefully enough the plight of the non-scholar of ancient languages. The specialists are happy to be given the job of making judgments, and often good ones, about the meanings of the words in ancient manuscripts. They have access to those Hebrew and Greek words. I do not have that same access. I believe they can help me most effectively through books and commentaries that explain the cultural contexts and issues of meaning while allowing me as full access as possible to the literal words—i.e., an essentially literal translation, such as the English Standard Version.

If the Hebrew text of Proverbs 13:1 most literally reads, "A wise son hears his father's instruction" (ESV), then I want to know that, rather than being given words such as, "A wise child heeds a parent's instruction" (TNIV). The scholars can help me with the background of Proverbs and its cultural context; it will not be difficult to figure out that this principle of sons obeying fathers does indeed apply to children and parents. The role of sons in ancient times and the nature of their training for leadership are actually quite interesting to look into. Moreover, Proverbs has much to say, quite literally, about the roles of both fathers and mothers in child-rearing, so that even just a careful reading of the entire book will hone my understanding.

If the Hebrew text says most literally that "David slept with his fathers and was buried in the city of David" (1 Kings 2:10 ESV), then I want to know that, rather than being given the words, "David died and was buried with his ancestors in the city of David" (NLT). "Slept with his fathers" is a metaphor, a picture of death, a picture actually rich in layers of meaning when you think about it. We'll talk further about metaphor. Why should we close off that richness in an attempt to help the reader by means of translation, as opposed to good writing and teaching?

I recommend Leland Ryken's discussion of these issues, with the caveat that his two excellent books are all for essentially literal as opposed to dynamic-equivalency translation.[4] Gordon Fee and Mark Strauss offer a helpful discussion from a somewhat different perspective, one held by many wonderful brothers and sisters in Christ.[5] The issue is crucial for all of us to consider.

Respect for the words of Scripture necessitates attention to translation and careful *observation*. We are not very good at observing words of text these days. We all know what it's like to jump from one Internet link to another without fully reading those on the way, much less stopping to observe them carefully. And, of course, we'll all choose different links and interpret differently the trail we follow! Before encouraging observation, it is important to acknowledge again that none of us brings a totally objective mind or heart to a text; we all have those individual contexts and experiences through which we see the dance of words coming across the bridge.

However, along with acknowledging subjectivity, we also have been affirming a meaning to the biblical text, a meaning originally intended by God who breathed it out and carried along the writers, who caught that intention and worked out just the right words. From God emanated the whole dance to begin with. Otherwise, words couldn't be or mean at all. Meaning depends on him. The next chapter will deal with our attempt to move closer and closer to the intended meaning of a biblical text. This chapter is dealing with the initial step of receiving the words with careful attention. It is often our nonobservant approach to a text that allows our subjective viewpoints to overpower the words.

I'll never forget the pastors' retreats my husband and I enjoyed during his time on the pastoral staff at College Church in Wheaton. There was plenty of fun and food and games and sharing of lives in all kinds of ways. In the mornings, each staff person and spouse was given a paper with the same long Scripture passage printed on it. We spent at least an hour individually, prayerfully reading and rereading the passage, noticing things about it, and marking it up. We were given no helps at this stage. The senior pastor, Kent Hughes, would have done his homework and was ready to lead and teach with all the necessary background when the time came for discussion. Every new staff person (and spouse!) was intimidated to some degree by this group exercise . . . until we simply embraced the joy of it. What a privilege: uninterrupted time with just the Word of God in front of us and passionate fellow lovers of the Word with whom to discuss it—for hours, if we wanted.

The initial stage of observation should be full of possibility and openness. It is truly amazing what can happen when we take the time to make specific observations about a passage. I have increasingly come to believe that it is often not helpful to begin right away with a set list of questions because each passage and each book works differently and elicits unique observation, especially at the start. People are often intimidated by this initial stage of observation; they feel they have a void to fill, and they're not qualified. Here's where trust in the living and active nature of the words makes a difference, perhaps especially for the leader who risks laying out that void and watching the group disappear into it.

"Have a copy of the text on paper. Unless you really like marking your Bible, you can print the text from a number of software programs. Leave a wide margin (3–4 inches) for jotting down your observations. Assign a tentative title (a word or short phrase) to each paragraph in the passage. Personally, this is a step I never skip because it results in my having my first glimpse of the point of the passage."

—JoAnn Cairns, Bible study author and teacher,
College Church in Wheaton, Illinois

I often encourage students of the Word to begin by reading nonstop through a long passage or a whole book. Reading out loud can be especially helpful. Then, on rereading, observations begin to emerge: repeated words, intriguing phrases, themes, pictures, shapes of lines or paragraphs . . . all the things we will come back to in more detail in the process of a careful study. But the first step of observation is crucial. I've heard students ask Leland Ryken how he finds what he finds in the texts of Scripture. I've heard him answer: "Well, first I read it. And then I read it again. And then I read it again . . ." I've often heard my husband quote advice he read in graduate school concerning how to deal with a certain complex philosophical work: "Keep staring at the page until random acts of understanding occur." I don't recommend just staring. But I do recommend spending a lot of initial time reading and observing.

In a recent study of Psalms with a women's group at my church, I was amazed by what happened at the opening of every session as we simply shared initial observations we had written down before moving into the study questions. Of course, we got better and better at this stage each week, as we became more comfortable and as our observations began to grow and take into account all the psalms of the weeks before. Throughout our lives we grow in our ability to observe a biblical text. But we can do it at any and every stage of our experience. We can learn from each other by doing it together.

As we arrived at Psalm 98 in that group study, I recall opening to the psalm in my preparation and feeling a leader's common fear that this text (which on first blush looks like sort of a generic praise psalm) might elicit absolutely no comments from anybody. I needed to do my observation and study. I came ready and armed. However, when the group gathered, they came bursting with observations about the "noisiness" of the psalm . . . its travel to so many places in its praise . . . the absence of that depressed "I" we had seen in previous psalms . . . the people-praise and then the nature-praise sections of the psalm . . . the parallel lines of verse 2, which begin to reveal salvation's plan . . . the intriguing climax of God's judgment. . . . The comments were themselves a litany of praise in response to the psalm's own praise. The living and active words did their work in our group!

Sufficiency of the Words

If God's Word is alive and active and powerful, then, first, we should study it with respect for the words. Second, we should study it trusting in the sufficiency of the words—without itching for something else. Such a powerful Word is a sufficient Word. Peter tells us that God's "divine power has granted to us all things that pertain to life and godliness, through the knowledge of him who called us to his own glory and excellence, by which he has granted to us his precious and very great promises" (2 Peter 1:3–4). Everything . . . all things we need for life and godliness are ours in Christ, who brings to completion every promise God has ever made, every word he has ever spoken.

The sufficiency of this Word, as it reveals the sufficiency of Christ, should keep us from being the kind of people with "itching ears," who "will not endure sound teaching" but who "will accumulate for themselves teachers to suit their own passions, and will turn away from listening to the truth and wander off into myths" (2 Tim. 4:3–4). Paul tells Timothy in that passage to "preach the word" and not to be put off by people who want something else or something more.

This is a good reminder for anybody in ministry, including people in Bible study, which can seem mundane sometimes, or hard, or long. Words take a great deal of attention and energy . . . wouldn't it be more fun to do something more entertaining? Or wouldn't it be easier just to bring in a dynamic speaker, live or recorded, to "make these words come alive" for us? Or wouldn't it be nice if God would just speak directly to us from time to time, instead of making us dig into this book?

"Seeing God transform people through his Word has been the most exciting thing I have witnessed. I love working and teaching and training women to do this; there is nothing more gratifying than seeing people's progress over years, steadily moving from very little understanding to clarity and deep, abiding faith and understanding. . . . I have seen self-preoccupied, sad women learn the joy and love of Christ through reading the Scriptures. I have seen new believers grow to be teachers of other women. I have seen some of the wobbliest thinkers become clear and keen. I have seen women weep in gratitude because their hunger for God's Word is being satisfied. What a privilege. There have been heartbreaks as well: people continuing in lazy habits, or walking away into disobedient choices or just disinterest."

—Bron Short, Bible study leader and writer, St. John's Shaughnessy, Vancouver, British Columbia, Canada

---

Several years ago a beautiful young woman began to attend a church Bible study I was helping to lead. She was a single mom raising a lovely little sprite of a toddler girl with long, curly, dark hair just like her mother. Just a few sessions into the study, I noticed this young woman sitting there with tears streaming down her cheeks, despair in her face. The two of us slipped into the adjoining kitchen to talk, and the woman explained through sobs that she felt at the end of herself, trying to make ends meet and struggling to raise this little girl alone. She poured out to me her story of how the night before she had lain on her bed with her daughter in her arms and pleaded for God to speak to her and to give her just one little word of comfort or guidance. She looked at me and through her tears said, "I waited and waited, and he didn't speak to me. He didn't answer."

In our Bible study we had recently begun to study the book of Hebrews. This young woman and I sat down together and went back to the first chapter of that book, to the opening where it says that in the past, in many different times and ways, God spoke to his people directly, through the prophets. That would have included all kinds of dreams and visions and direct speaking. But, verse 2 continues, in these last days (which is now) he has spoken to us by his Son. He *has spoken* to us! He's given us Jesus—the culmination of his word to us, which is now complete. David Jackman puts it rather strongly: "Beyond Christ, God has nothing more to say."[6] Or we might say that in Christ God has fully revealed his word, to which nothing more can be added or subtracted.

I was able to tell this young woman that God had indeed answered her, had indeed spoken to her, was indeed speaking to her, in Christ and through his Word. She began to attend church and Bible study regularly, and she began to listen and hear God speaking to her. His powerful Word came through and met her need with sufficiency. She began to connect with other people who were listening, and I believe she is still connected and listening today.

I would draw no conclusion about God's ways of speaking to people who do not have his Word. Most often, I think, he brings it to them through translators and preachers and missionary-hearted disciples with the beautiful feet of those who bring good news. I would, however, draw conclusions about those of us who do have his Word but who look for something more or something else for life and godliness. God has given us his living and active Word, and through it he pours out to us his full salvation in Jesus Christ. The gift comes, strangely enough, through a book of powerful words that we do well to receive—and to help others receive—with great respect and confidence as we approach them for study.

As a little girl I was given a Halley's *Pocket Bible Handbook,* a little study guide to the Scriptures, at the beginning of which appears this quotation from D. L. Moody:

> I prayed for faith, and thought that some day faith would come down and strike me like lightning. But faith did not seem to come.
>
> One day I read in the tenth chapter of Romans, "Now faith comes by hearing, and hearing by the Word of God." I had closed my Bible, and prayed for faith. I now opened my Bible and began to study, and faith has been growing ever since.[7]

3

If the Bible Is Understandable . . .

Then How Should We Get It?

Truth №3: The Bible is understandable.

Implications for study:

1. Finding the main idea
2. Asking questions (chapter 4)

The Bible Is Understandable

If we affirm meaning in the text, meaning intended by God who breathed it out, then it follows that God means for us to receive this meaning. He gave us words that he evidently means for us to understand. We have talked about careful reading and observation of the words as the first step. But that step leads to others, others that will help us more and more faithfully receive the meaning that God intends for us to receive through these words. I suppose we will all arrive at exactly the right meaning when we see Jesus face-to-face and the life and meaning of the Word burst on us fully. Until that time we can keep studying, getting closer, and nurturing the attitude of prayerful humility that admits that we imperfect creatures, even to begin to understand, need the help of God through his Holy Spirit, who inspired these words in the first place.

It becomes more and more complicated to talk about the steps of study because they are all interrelated. This chapter depends on the following chapters that discuss the literary genres and the unified story of Scripture. All these truths and implications in the end must work together. But it is important to establish at the start the principle of a biblical text's understandability, although we will have to refine and re-refine this principle and its implications as we move along.

The claim that the Bible is understandable is a very old claim. The Reformers of the sixteenth century, for example, based their lives' work on the fact that they could study Scripture for its clear meaning, meaning that was being contradicted by the church of that day. The Roman Catholic Church viewed the Scriptures as dark and obscure, claiming that interpretation must be left to the pope and the authoritative body of church tradition. Martin Luther, in *Bondage of the Will,* wrote almost ferociously about the perspicuity (clarity) of Scripture, accusing those who claimed that the Bible lacks plain meaning of being used by Satan "to scare men off reading the sacred text, and to destroy all sense of its value." Just a sentence later Luther goes on to admit that "many passages in the Scriptures are obscure and hard to elucidate," but, he claims, "that is due, not to the exalted nature of their subject, but to our own linguistic and grammatical ignorance." And just a couple of sentences later he explains that a more obscure passage must be explained by other more clear ones.[1]

The Westminster divines considered this truth of the basic clarity of Scripture important enough to include in their Westminster Confession of 1647, Chapter 1, Article VII—again with a humble acknowledgment of the Bible's complexity along with its basic clarity:

> All things in Scripture are not alike plain in themselves, nor alike clear unto all: yet those things which are necessary to be known, believed, and observed for salvation are so clearly propounded, and opened in some place of Scripture or other, that not only the learned, but the unlearned, in a due use of the ordinary means, may attain unto a sufficient understanding of them.

But we should go back further, to the testimony of Scripture concerning itself. We have seen its affirmation of its God-breathed source, and of its power to make wise for salvation, to pierce hearts with its living and active truth, and to be profitable for everything needed in order to learn and teach godliness to the end. Such claims seem simply to assume the transmission and reception of meaningful, effectual words. The consistent images of light to picture the Word reinforce this sense: Peter spoke of the prophetic word as that "lamp shining in a dark place" (2 Peter 1:19), and the psalmist calls God's word "a lamp to my feet and a light to my path" (Ps. 119:105). What an encouragement: Scripture itself leads us to expect our way to be lighted up with the illumination of understanding, as we take it in more and more deeply.

One delightful aspect of Scripture's own witness to its understandability is its urging to read it to the simple. It's complex, but it's not just for smart intellectuals. God wants everybody to read it and understand it as fully as possible. Many know that familiar passage in Deuteronomy 6, in which God commands that his words be on the people's hearts, that they shall teach them diligently to their children, talking of them while sitting at home, walking, lying down, and rising. Every parent (and every believer with influence over young people in one way or another . . . in other words, all of us!) has been given the momentous job of teaching the Bible to the next generation, talking about it all the time, showing its relevance to everything we're thinking and doing. There's almost no better argument for not leaving biblical study to the professionals. One has to have studied the complexities in order to distill them for a child or a youth into simple and not simplistic form. On the basis of Scripture itself we can be confident that there is much—more than we often think—that even a child can understand.

One of my favorite pictures of the Word's being communicated with clarity to everybody appears in the book of Nehemiah, at the point where the returned exiles have finished rebuilding the walls of Jerusalem. Recall this stunningly beautiful, crowded scene:

> And all the people gathered as one man into the square before the Water Gate. And they told Ezra the scribe to bring the Book of the Law of Moses that the LORD had commanded Israel. So Ezra the priest brought the Law before the assembly, both men and women and all who could understand what they heard, on the first day of the seventh month. And he read from it facing the square before the Water Gate from early morning until midday, in the presence of the men and the women and

those who could understand. And the ears of all the people were attentive to the Book of the Law. (Neh. 8:1–3)

That repeated phrase, "men and women and all who could understand," drives home the comprehensive audience that God intends for his Word, probably here including many children and young people.

Another encouragement to be found in this scene is that the Levite leaders moved through the crowd and "helped the people to understand the Law. . . . They read from the book, from the Law of God, clearly, and they gave the sense, so that the people understood the reading" (Neh. 8:7–8). These teachers "gave the sense," that is, explained the meaning of the words. And the people *understood!* They probably did not understand perfectly, but clearly enough that this passage itself actually affirms their understanding. In fact, this understanding is reemphasized when we're told later that they went away rejoicing "because they had understood the words that were declared to them" (8:12).

I don't know of a clearer picture of God's people gathered together for the purpose of taking in and understanding his Word. There are leaders and teachers to help, and that is good and necessary. In another scene of guided understanding, centuries later, Philip asked that Ethiopian eunuch, "Do you understand what you are reading?" The eunuch responded, "How can I, unless someone guides me?" Philip guided him, and he understood, was baptized, and also "went on his way rejoicing" (see Acts 8:26–39).

When in Psalm 119:130 the psalmist praises God that "the unfolding of your words gives light; it imparts understanding to the simple," he perhaps refers not only to someone intellectually simple (like a child), but also to someone not mature in the ways of wisdom. God's Word can bring the light of understanding to both, by the power of the Spirit. Jesus actually rebukes many foolish people who know the Scriptures but refuse to receive understanding from them; the problem is not with the Scriptures, but with the people's hard hearts. In Matthew 12:1–8, Jesus reproaches the Pharisees, specialists in the Law, with the repeated ironic phrase, "Have you not read . . . ?" He quotes Hosea and says they do not know the meaning of Hosea's words. They have shut out the light of understanding, evidenced by the fact that they shut their hearts against Jesus himself, the one to whom all the Scriptures point.

"In reaching out to Muslims, study of the Scriptures is vital. In 2 Timothy 3:15, Paul writes that the Scriptures 'are able to make you wise for salvation through faith in Christ Jesus.' Mahmoud e-mailed our church because he wanted to know more about Christianity. My husband hooked this young man up with another elder, and the two studied the Scriptures together. Mahmoud is now doing an internship with our church, studying to become a pastor."

—Keri Folmar, pastor's wife and Bible study teacher, United Christian Church of Dubai, United Arab Emirates

---

As we study, opening our hearts and our minds by the power of the Spirit is essential. Indeed, the dual aspects of God's working and our working must both be emphasized, as we affirm the possibility of understanding his Word. The light does not usually just break on people when they get close to the Word. The people in Nehemiah showed up at the break of dawn and stood there for a long time. To assert the perspicuity of Scripture is most certainly not to say that understanding it is easy. Parts of it are especially hard to understand, and studying any part of it takes work. To study the Bible takes time and effort, and most of us today are simply not in the habit of giving such time and effort to any kind of challenging texts.

"The most difficult problem is hardened hearts that no longer love God's Word above the things of this world. Too few value God's insistence on knowing him through his Word, the importance of holiness, the necessity of wisdom, the reality of daily spiritual warfare, or the fruits in ourselves and God's kingdom of knowing the Word."

—Diane Poythress, Ph.D., teacher, founder of Women's Weekend Seminary, Lansdale Presbyterian Church, Lansdale, Pennsylvania

---

Timothy Larsen describes the common reading habits of Victorian England, where children were raised on the King James Version of the Bible, which was read daily and comprehensively in their homes and taught as the primary text in their education. "One could not gain a bachelor's degree in any subject from the University of Oxford without first passing an examination on Holy Scripture, the Gospels portion of which was on the original Greek text."[2] Larsen goes on to posit that because people were routinely trained in reading Scripture—with its complex array of literary genres, its historical and cultural scope, and its diverse vocabulary—they were thereby enabled to be proficient readers of all kinds of "hard" literature. Common laborers were in the habit of picking up cheap pocket copies of great writers, like Homer and Pliny, and digesting them happily and easily.

Affirming the Bible's understandability implies not only that God has offered us words whose meaning we can increasingly grasp, but also that we are called to give ourselves to the work of grasping that meaning. We're seriously out of the habit. Dedicated Bible study can help restore that habit so that we can walk more and more in the light of God's Word.

Implications

Finding the Main Idea

The implications of the Bible's understandability involve steps of labor, steps that help us work our way into the meaning of a text after the initial reading and observation. The first implication is the necessity of finding the main idea of a text—what it's primarily about. This starting point itself is a radical one, as many groups might rather start by sharing what the text "means to me." What if we start by trying first to grasp the meaning that God through the authors intended—because we believe there is meaning to be understood? How can we properly personalize or apply words before we understand basically what they say? We must continually affirm the existence of personal contexts and biases that will affect our understanding, but we can work against the domination of those personal contexts and biases by stopping to ask questions of the text—first concerning its main idea.

For the purposes of this discussion, I will assume that the text being studied is part of a whole biblical book being studied. Further discussion will make it increasingly clear why studies of whole biblical books (as opposed to studies using collections of scattered verses) in general offer the most profit from our regular study of the Scriptures. The Bible as one whole book has a main idea, which we will get to and which we must always get to. But each book within the whole also has a main idea, as well as particular sections within books. Some call the main idea a "melodic line"—a helpful image of the notes of a melody stretching through and uniting a whole work from beginning to end.[3] Before attempting to identify the main idea of any section within a book, it is best to identify the main idea of the book, for each of its sections will relate to that big idea in some way.

"Perhaps the least effective method of Bible study I've experienced is for a group of people to get together, read a passage, and share with each other 'what this passage means to me.' This actually denies the fact that the Bible has any concrete meaning at all. It simply means what each person wants it to mean."

—Carol Ruvolo, author and Bible study leader, Heritage Christian Fellowship, Albuquerque, New Mexico

---

After careful reading and observation, one is ready to begin to think about the big idea of a book. What is the book mainly about? Is there one idea that flows through and unites the different sections? Is there a melody that keeps appearing in various forms and developments like a main theme in a piece of music? To land on a main idea, it is helpful to read again the beginning and ending sections of the book: is there a concept that seems to tie it all together from top to bottom? Are there repeating words or phrases throughout the book that relate to this main idea? Does the main idea we're trying out as a possibility seem to make sense of the different sections throughout the book?

"In a recent teacher training course for women (small-group leaders, teachers, and mothers), as we worked through various assignments in learning how to study the Bible, I realized that many jumped right over what the passage actually said and went straight to some personal application they derived . . . rather than digging into the actual text first so that the application was drawn from it. I was reminded of our tendency to approach Scripture saying, 'What's in it for me?' rather than 'What does this say?'"

—Donna Dobbs, Director of Christian Education, First Presbyterian Church, Jackson, Mississippi

---

The easiest example to use is the gospel of John—although John is not an easy book! However, we get the main idea easily because John hands it to us. We do have to read the whole book to find it because he doesn't announce it until John 20:30–31, which concludes with the reason he has written the book: "so that you may believe that Jesus is the Christ, the Son of God, and that by believing you may have life in his name."

The stated aim of the book here encompasses the main idea, which is something like: "believing in Jesus Christ and finding life." However you state it, *believing* has to be central, because as you read the book, the word *believe* comes up regularly and not just randomly; believing (or not believing) seems to be the point of most of the passages. It is the point of the climactic passage right before John 20:30–31, in which Thomas says he won't believe and then finally believes. But we will want to include "Jesus the Christ" in the main idea because *who he is*, right from the start, is the key. Who he is *is* what we must believe. I think that *life* also should be included in the main idea because the life we receive through believing in Christ is the gift that continues to be offered, pictured, and promised throughout the book. Clearly, there is not one set way to state a main idea; we should work to grasp a main idea more and more clearly.

Consider 1 Thessalonians: what's the main idea in that challenging little book? Paul addresses many subjects as he writes to these people to whom he was able to preach the gospel. The initial "triad" in 1 Thessalonians 1:3 is well known, as Paul celebrates their "work of faith and labor of love and steadfastness of hope." Reading the whole epistle, we come to recognize that repeated gospel shape, which moves from initial faith in Christ all the way to the end we hope for—the return of Christ to this earth. That shape, and especially the hope of its culmination, governs the epistle. We might say that the main idea is how to live the gospel in light of the end. Chapter 1 ends with the idea of waiting for the Son from heaven. Chapter 2 ends with Paul's anticipation of "boasting" in these believers at Jesus' coming. Chapter 3 ends with Paul's prayer that they will be "blameless in holiness . . . at the coming of our Lord Jesus with all his saints." Chapter 4 ends with the picture of being caught up to meet the Lord in the air, when he comes with his saints. Chapter 5 ends with another prayer similar to that of chapter 3. The way each section ends with that look ahead reminds us of the way each section, each day, each portion of our lives should be marked with that same focus and hope.

What about an Old Testament book like Joshua? The main subject matter of the book is Joshua's leading God's people into the Promised Land. But the book begins with God's words to Joshua about the importance of remembering and keeping God's unfailing words (now in the form of a written Law, received through Moses, who has just died). And the book ends with a final speech in which Joshua admonishes the people to remember God's unfailing words that they have seen fulfilled and to obey God's words as they enter the Promised Land. There seems to be a melodic line at work. The main idea of Joshua, we might conclude, should include an acknowledgment of God's ongoing covenant promises being fulfilled in the "inheritance" (a word that appears often) of the land of rest God gives to his people. We'll stop at that point and come back later to Joshua because its main idea connects to the whole Bible's main idea. It's hard to talk about the main idea of Joshua without talking about this book's place in the unfolding revelation of God in Scripture. We'll get there. But we've begun to get there.

I've tried to talk about this concept of main idea with a certain amount of flexibility. People can often articulate a main idea a number of different ways, and good Bible students may even disagree. We may grow in our understanding of a book over time and come to refine our sense of its main idea. Many, for example, would say that the main idea of Philippians is gospel *joy*. I've heard some say it is gospel *partnership*. Maybe it's a combination of those two concepts. Perhaps the *ESV Study Bible*'s suggestion actually combines these two concepts when it tells us in the introduction to the book that "the chief theme of Philippians is encouragement."[4] One can see even in the midst of such discussions that the discussions can help hone an understanding of the main idea, especially if the point is to keep returning to the text to see if it all fits.

Once we've begun to get a sense of a book's main idea, then each section or passage in the book will make more sense, as its own smaller main idea relates to the whole book's main idea and develops it in some way. For example, when we get to the final instructions of Paul in 1 Thessalonians 5:12–22, how should we attempt to state a main idea for this passage? Should we just treat it as a random parting grocery list? Should we study it by treating each separate command (there are over a dozen) in isolation, using lots of cross-references? Or should we examine these commands together as Paul's concluding word on how a body of believers should live when they have Jesus' second coming properly in mind? They are relational commands, commands for the bride of Christ as she prepares to meet her groom. Indeed, all subjects addressed in various passages throughout this book, such as work, sexual holiness, and church order, are addressed in light of preparing for that day when we meet Jesus. So as we get down to the level of studying the words and the phrases of the various passages, examining vocabulary and grammar and logic, we can do this detailed work with an eye to how the passage fits within the book.

When we study to get a book's main idea, and the various passages' main ideas in light of the book's main idea, then we won't feel we are moving in a different direction with each subsequent passage. We won't be making lots of short trips, but one long one with a number of segments. This thematic or "big-idea" approach works quite well even with the different genres we will discuss. And as a person trained to analyze literary texts in general, I must say that it works especially well with the books of the Bible because they are masterfully written, each with a unified idea beautifully developed. This unity of focus is indeed one of the marks of great writing. God has given us the most excellent examples through the writers and the writings he inspired.

"When we teach or study, we often jump in feet first and say, 'What is in it for me, now?'—without taking time to look at content . . . context . . . historical redemptive focus . . . and finally, application. We tend to jump to stories and application too soon, without taking time to marinate in the surrounding territory of the Scriptures and to do so meditatively."

—Kari Stainback, Director of Women's Ministries, Park Cities Presbyterian Church, Dallas, Texas

---

The second implication of the fact that Scripture is understandable is that we should keep asking questions in order to understand. Those further questions will be the focus of the next chapter.

4

Asking Questions . . .

A Second Implication

THE BIBLE IS UNDERSTANDABLE—that's the truth affirmed
in the previous chapter. That truth brought us to the first
implication: we should search out the main idea of a biblical
text. The question of the main idea is indeed the first question to ask. But if this truth is really true, then the text will
be sturdy enough to stand up to other questions. That's the
second implication: we should *keep asking questions*. Students
of the Bible have to be indefatigable question askers.

In Bible study material that is "out there," we find many
possible and many helpful lists of questions people use to
make their way into a text. A good number use variations of
the Who, What, When, Where, How, and Why questions. I
like to use a set of questions that I originally encountered in
different form at College Church in Wheaton through the
visiting workshops of R. C. Lucas (of St. Helen's Church,
Bishopsgate, London). The Charles Simeon Trust preaching
and teaching workshops are his American offspring, in a sense,

and they bear the imprint of his remarkable instruction and modeling of biblical study and exposition.[1] These questions, though originating from Dick Lucas, have evolved at College Church and elsewhere over the years. I have added one, the third of now Seven Questions. They represent one possible route of questioning that will lead us deeper into the meaning of a text. Here is the list, followed by brief comments on each question.

Seven Questions to Ask of a Text

1. Crux?
2. Context?
3. Configuration?
4. Characters?
5. Christ?
6. Curiosities?
7. Conclusions?

1. Crux

Yes, they all begin with *c*—which is, I think, the explanation for this word *crux*, a bit of an unusual word for many people. *Crux* simply means the main idea, the question we discussed in the last chapter. This is indeed the first question to ask.

2. Context

The *context* question asks us to examine what surrounds any word, verse, passage, or book under examination. The largest textual context, of course, is the whole biblical story, and we will get to that. It is usually most helpful to deal with the context question by starting closer in and moving farther out, that is, by moving from the *immediate context,* to the *whole-book context,* and then to the *whole-biblical context.* Along with these textual considerations must come attention to the *cultural and historical context.*

"For the churched, often the Bible has been learned in verses or 'bumper-sticker segments' so that people are not as able to approach the Bible as a whole. They often don't care about context, which has a great deal to do with how something is understood and interpreted. Many well-churched people come to the Bible not to discover, but to confirm currently held beliefs and understandings, so they 'read into' it."

—anonymous pastor, serving in East Asia

The immediate context of a word or verse or passage is simply the words or verses or passages that come right before and after. Let's go back to 1 Thessalonians to see how this context question works and builds on the crux question. Reading a discrete passage (one that can stand alone) like 1 Thessalonians 4:1–12, we would probably say that this section's main idea is something like the call for moral purity within the church. But can we study this passage in isolation? We have said that any passage's main idea should relate to the main idea of the book, rather than being just an isolated topic. Examining the immediate context can help.

If we read the passages before and after this one (1 Thess. 3:11–13 and 4:13–18), we notice that our passage is embedded in talk of the Lord's second coming, that main idea that seems to dominate the whole book. Strong talk of Jesus' appearing looms over this passage on both sides, and that must affect its meaning. The immediate context of this passage leads us to believe that Paul is urging moral purity *so that* God might "establish your hearts blameless in holiness before our God and Father, at the coming of our Lord Jesus with all his saints" (1 Thess. 3:13). This is about not just a holy life, but a holy life in light of the end. Clearly, the immediate context connects to the whole-book context—which is why it is important to begin with that "crux" question and never leave it behind.

The context question helps us understand the Epistles, where, in general, teaching on holy living comes in the context of teaching on the theological truth of the gospel. We might go astray even as the Colossian Christians were tempted to do, for example, if we took Paul's instruction starting in Colossians 2:6 without connecting that instruction to the preceding passages, where he explains the person and the gospel of the Lord Jesus Christ. Colossians' first passages develop utterly logically into the later ones, as we see in the logic and grammar of key transitional sentences: "Therefore, as you received Christ," he says (Col. 2:6), and "If then you have been raised with Christ" (Col. 3:1). The context of the theological teaching is connected as with an umbilical cord to the later context of the practical implications—reminding us of James's warning that faith without works is dead (James 2:17).

Indeed, the temptation to extract a moral teaching from its context is huge, as we perhaps too quickly look for either lessons or support of a point we're trying to make. Does John 10:10, for example, make an argument against abortion? ("I came that they may have life and have it abundantly.") The context will answer that question: who's speaking, and to whom does he refer as "they"? What is the main point of the passage where this statement is found? What kind of life is being pictured here? This "Good Shepherd passage" is essentially about salvation, and Jesus as the door into it, which "they," being his sheep, are called to enter. Yes, we might say that Jesus is "pro-life," but we should certainly hesitate to use this passage as a proof text for the pro-life movement.

I recall a teaching from Malachi 3:6–15, in which the teacher addressed the topic of tithing and the blessing that comes from giving generously to the Lord. The focus moved from physical to spiritual giving, so that we were encouraged to give not just our physical goods but our whole lives in response to a God who gave himself to us when he opened the windows of heaven and sent his Son. This was an important and beautiful acknowledgment of the whole-biblical context. However, there was no notice of the passages immediately before and after (Mal. 3:1–5 and 3:16–4:3), both of which vividly announce the coming day of the Lord's judgment. How are the coming "refiner's fire" of Malachi 3:2 and the burning oven of Malachi 4:1 important to our perspective on what is or is not eternally valuable? Why is this passage on tithing encased in such flaming heat?

In this example from Malachi, immediate-context questions again connect with whole-book-context questions. How does this burning concept of tithing fit into Malachi's whole prophetic message? Is there a main idea in Malachi relating to a proper response to God's judgment (and mercy)? We need to get a sense of the whole book in order to deal fully with this passage. Attention to the immediate context here also points the way to the whole-biblical context. " 'Behold, I send my messenger, and he will prepare the way before me,' " says the LORD in Malachi 3:1. Who is that messenger, and how does this announcement of him fit not only into the book but also into the whole big story?

Along with such textual-context questions, we must ask the historical- and cultural-context questions—not about the words but about the *worlds* surrounding the text. What was going on in the relatively new body of believers in Thessalonica? What false teachings in the church at Colossae was Paul trying to address? What were the cultures of those cities like? At what time in the history of Israel was Malachi prophesying? Malachi was a postexilic prophet, and so we need to learn what was happening among the returned exiles and among the nations all around them. Help in answering comes from other parts of Scripture, biblical dictionaries, books about various historical periods, and selected commentaries, all used to deal with questions that arise from the text itself.

A text, rather than filling in all the blanks, often seems to invite us to ask and answer such questions. Nehemiah, for example, revealing the postexilic history from another perspective, tells us immediately in first person that as he served as cupbearer to the king in the court of Susa, the capital, he received information about the Jews who had escaped from the exile to Jerusalem. Capital of what? Who was the king, when did he reign, and what was his court like? What did it mean to be his cupbearer? Who were the Jews who had survived what exile? Why were they in Jerusalem and Nehemiah in Susa? Answers to these questions open up this story of Nehemiah's leading the Jews who returned to rebuild the walls of Jerusalem after Persia's domination ended the Babylonian exile. The point in Bible study is to let our research into history and culture illumine the meaning of the text, not become itself the point of our study.

When we're studying Ruth, we will want to learn about the period of the judges in the history of Israel, about Moabites and the Jews' attitudes toward them, about Bethlehem, about

Jewish laws concerning the poor and foreigners and widows. We'll want to learn all this so that we will understand this book not in terms of the way we today would experience a love encounter between a man and a woman, but first of all in terms of the way it would have been experienced in the context of those people in that time and place. Studying the historical and cultural context sometimes sounds or feels like an intellectual exercise, but in fact it involves a humble opening of ourselves to a story that is bigger than the little contexts where each of us lives.

David I. Smith writes about cultural openness as an evidence of godly love for one's neighbor:

> Learning about another culture can become an exercise in intelligence gathering so as to secure my own advantage, or in collecting exotica to add to my mental museum of interesting facts, or in filling notebooks and polishing my brain in order to enhance my academic or economic prospects, or in listing comparisons that always end with the conclusion that my own ways are better. At least some of these motives have their place, but they may have little to do with love of God or neighbor. However, the same learning can be part of a process of making space within ourselves for others by attending respectfully and openheartedly to their stories and experiences. When this happens, even book learning can become a way of practicing "care taken with the lives and thoughts of others." Such learning becomes fitting preparation for the kinds of direct encounter with others that show love of my neighbor.[2]

There is definitely a kind of humility involved in "making space within ourselves" for stories of people from times and places different from our own. Keeping such aims and attitudes at the heart of Bible study can revolutionize both personal preparation and group interaction. At the heart of this kind of openness is the humble openness to hear God speaking—God who directs all the stories of all history and culture.

"With children, I bring in photos, archaeological data, books, videos, and items that can be handled (such as papyrus paper), to reinforce the actuality of place and time. Everyone's faith is encouraged, both young and old, when historical corroborations are unveiled. Children are tempted to think of the Bible as just another book, especially if it is among their assigned school books. I always teach them that this book is different from every other book because it was written by God and because it is alive. It can change your heart right now. It can reach inside of you because it is empowered by the Holy Spirit."

—Diane Poythress, Ph.D., teacher, founder of Women's Weekend Seminary, Lansdale Presbyterian Church, Lansdale, Pennsylvania

---

3. Configuration

The question of context works alongside the next question, the question of *configuration*. How is the passage (and the book it is part of) configured or put together? Often the initial stage of observation lays the groundwork for this question, as matters of form and shape tend to stand out to us. If there's a repeated refrain, for example, in a psalm—one that perhaps seems to mark each section—then we are likely to notice that. To examine configuration is to ask, "What is the shape of these words, from beginning to end?"

This question raises the issue of biblical genres, which we will discuss more specifically. In general, noticing the shape and organization of any book or passage helps us to understand it. It helps to be able to see Colossians' move from theological to practical teaching; this is the shape of the book. Even within one passage—Colossians 1:15–23, for example—the shape of this specific theological teaching on the person of Christ moves beautifully from Jesus' exalted being in relation to God, to Jesus' connection of that being to his creation, ultimately through his work of reconciliation on the cross. In this passage is the very shape of the gospel.

The configuration of a narrative always helps us understand the aim of the writer. Joshua's move from the death of Moses at the beginning to the death of Joshua at the end gives us a clue about the message of the ongoing covenant promises of God, generation after generation. (It also connects the narrative to the larger biblical story.) We can learn much from Joshua's arrangement of his scenes, as the whole large invasion story periodically stops and focuses in on personal encounters (for example, of Rahab and the spies in chapter 2, or of Joshua and that commander of the Lord's army in chapter 4) where the nature of God's promises is made vivid to individuals. The whole large story pauses periodically as well simply to reiterate the steadfastness of God's promises. We earlier saw the emphasis on God's unfailing word in both the book's beginning and ending speeches, but a careful reading will find that emphasis regularly throughout. Consider, for example, Joshua 11:16–23, where Joshua pauses to sum up the main conquest section of the book, celebrating the inheritance of the land given to Israel "according to all that the LORD had spoken to Moses."

The configuration of a poem offers huge insight into its meaning. In fact, for a discrete poem like a psalm, the question of configuration might come helpfully before the question of context. Of course, the context of the whole book of Psalms as the prayer-and-praise book of God's worshiping people is important to each psalm—as well as the immediate contexts for passages within a psalm. However, it doesn't usually help as much to notice the prior and the subsequent psalms as to notice the shape of a psalm itself. In Psalm 77, for example, one observes a movement from many uses of the first-person pronoun *I* in the first half, to many uses of the second-person pronoun *you* in the second half. When we read it, we feel a turning point somewhere in the middle (probably v. 10), as the tone seems to change. The psalmist moves from dark, lonely despair in the first section to a worshiping confidence found in contemplation of God's works on behalf of his people in the second. The poem's shape is crucial to its meaning: the lines show movement in two stages, movement that reflects what is happening in the psalmist's soul as he turns to God—and hopefully in our souls as we read it.

4. Characters

The question of *characters* lets us get at the meaning of a passage or a book by asking about the people involved in it. First of all, who wrote it, for whom, and from what perspective and situation? Who are the characters mentioned in the text? Is one central? With which one(s) do we identify and why?

Noting the characters can help unlock the meaning— as in the story of the prodigal son. According to the whole of Luke 15, when Jesus spoke this parable, to whom was he speaking, and to what charge was he responding? The chapter opens with the grumbling of the Pharisees and the scribes concerning the fact that Jesus "receives sinners and eats with them." The ensuing connected chain of three parables seems to respond directly to these grumbling characters. With which character in the parable of the prodigal son did Jesus mean to identify his listeners? With whom do we identify? What can we learn from the different characters in this parable? Why did the writer, Luke, choose to present this parable at this point in his gospel? All the characters involved are keys to understanding the meaning.

Not only narratives invite productive questions about characters. Even a book of love poetry like the Song of Solomon inspires extensive commentary concerning whether Solomon himself was the author or rather a representative main character, in what ways the author was reflecting the marriage customs and ceremonies of his time and place, whether in the poetry there are one or two male characters (just a king, who is pictured as a rustic shepherd—or a king and a rustic shepherd?) offering love to the woman, what might be the identities of the "daughters of Jerusalem," and so forth. Asking character questions opens up helpful routes into this biblical celebration of love between a man and a woman.

The movement of a character throughout a number of different scenes often communicates much. The story of Joseph comes to us in a shape that Scripture teaches us to know well, the shape of a **v**, which takes a character down to a deep, dark point of suffering, and then raises him from that point to a high place. We should watch for the meaning of this movement: in Joseph the movement shows not so much the development of the character himself as the providential hand of the gracious God in charge of the process. In the various gospel scenes featuring a character like Peter, however, we see great development from which we can learn much, as that fiery disciple moves from impulsive self-confidence to a final, humble believing in his Lord.

5. Christ

Where is *Christ* in this passage? How does this passage point us to Christ, the central character of all the Scriptures? You might say this is the central question of the Scriptures. We will devote chapters 7 and 8 to this question.

6. Curiosities

Curiosities means "surprises." What surprises do I find in the text before me? We so often think we know a passage well, but to look for surprises opens our eyes to new thoughts or words that we might not otherwise even notice. The presence of people new to the Scriptures makes this question come alive in a group. I recall, in a study on the gospel of John, hearing a woman who was reading John 1:1 for the first time talk about how strange and yet wonderful it was to call someone a "Word." I remember the sense of wonder that I was able to experience through her eyes, concerning a passage I knew so well that I hadn't explored the surprise of it nearly enough.

The example I often use for a curiosity is one I love, but I can't recall if it came to me in studying or if I learned it from someone else. If the latter is the case, perhaps whoever offered it to me will read this and remind me! The surprise comes after Joshua, in battle with the Amorites, prays and commands the sun to stand still, and it does. This is an amazing miracle. So when the text comments, "There has been no day like it

54

before or since, when . . ." what would we expect to read? I would expect to read something like, "when God changed the very courses of the planets." But the text concludes: "when the LORD heeded the voice of a man, for the LORD fought for Israel" (Josh. 10:12–14). The miracle we might expect to wonder at is eclipsed by the miracle of prayer—that God should listen to Joshua when he "spoke to the LORD" on behalf of his people. That's the miracle to wonder at here.

7. Conclusions

The question of *conclusions* asks what we will take away from the text and how we will apply it. This question comes rightly at the end. *Finally,* what does this text (now that I'm beginning to grasp what it means) mean to me, and what should I do with it? Because Scripture's words are indeed alive and active, conclusions and applications will emerge as we study them; we will not have to impose our conclusions and applications on the text.

If we're studying Joshua carefully, then our conclusions after many of those battle scenes probably won't be that God is promising to destroy our opponents in a ball game, a lawsuit, or even a just war. We will have grasped the story and the context in which these promises were given. Conclusions that grow from Joshua's main idea and its development throughout the book will probably have more to do with the nature of God's covenant word to his people, ultimately in Christ, and our call to trust and obey that word.

If we're studying the book of Esther carefully, then our conclusions will probably not center on the power of a strong woman in a male-dominated world, or even just the example of a courageous godly woman. Our conclusions will probably have more to do with God's providential ordering of events on behalf of his people, for his saving purposes, and our need to trust him in this ordering and for these purposes.

"One Sunday school class I recall used a Bible study curriculum with different passages of Scripture to study each week. One lesson dealt with John 6:1–15, the feeding of the five thousand. The focus was on the boy who gave his five loaves and two fish for Jesus to multiply for all those hungry people. The big application question for us to consider was: 'What do you have to give Jesus that he can multiply?' The well-intentioned study guide completely missed John's main point of showing Jesus to be the Creator God come in the flesh—just as he is proclaimed to be in John 1. When we study the Scriptures, we must not look for how to apply the passage to our lives before we figure out why the author wrote the passage—or the book. Application of our text must come out of the meaning of the text if we are truly applying the Scriptures, as opposed to our human ideas."

—Keri Folmar, pastor's wife and Bible study teacher, United Christian Church of Dubai, United Arab Emirates

---

If we're studying the book of Colossians carefully, then our conclusions won't focus just on the direct applications in the latter part of the book concerning legalism, or pure and impure attitudes of the heart, or relationships with the people around us. Our conclusions will include the theology of the earlier sections. That is, part of our "take-away" will be a deeper understanding of who Christ is and what he has done. Concluding applications do not involve only "action points"; they also involve embracing truth, which will change our hearts and our actions. Our conclusions will also include the ways that Paul calls us to live out this gospel truth about Christ, with regard to legalism, heart attitudes, and relationships.

These seven questions, or questions like them, will help us understand a Word that is understandable according to God's gracious plan. We should always be refining our questions. In fact, the next chapter will discuss ways of refining them according to the literary nature of the particular text in front of us.

5

≈

If the Bible Is a Literary Work . . .

Then What Should We Expect?

Truth №4: The Bible is a literary work.

Implications for study:

1. Reading for more than propositions
2. Relishing literary genres (continued in chapter 6)

The Bible Is a Literary Work

We've already used terms like *narrative* and *poem* because we can't even begin to observe the biblical text without noticing its literary aspects. In fact, in paying close attention to the words and the shape of a text, we have been talking consistently about literary matters; the Bible asks it of us. I would hope that my background in literature would enrich Bible study rather than impose on it a particular interpretive grid. The starting points of truths about the Scripture itself should help ensure that careful attention to everything about the Bible's words arises most fundamentally not from a commitment to literature but from a theologically based commitment to (and love of) the words God inspired.

If the Bible is indeed God speaking, then we do well to listen with full and utmost attention to every detail. If it is true that God is the original word-speaker and that every human being uses words only because of the image of God in him, then anything about words, including their literary beauty, has to do with God. We *all* (not just "literary people" but all of us) need to pay more attention to words.

It is true that over the last several decades there has been growing attention to the literary aspects of the Bible. Leland Ryken in 1987 spoke of a "quiet revolution going on in the study of the Bible," involving "a growing awareness that the Bible is a work of literature and that the methods of literary scholarship are a necessary part of any complete study of the Bible."[1] Ryken's own books have played their part; they offer an excellent introduction to the Bible's literary aspects.[2] It is true that many Scripture-lovers over the centuries who paid close attention to its words have been practicing a form of literary criticism, perhaps without the more technical language. But it is good to recognize that we are dealing with a literary text and to be intentional about literary questions.

The writer of Ecclesiastes was quite intentional about his writing process, which is described as follows:

> Besides being wise, the Preacher also taught the people knowl-
> edge, weighing and studying and arranging many proverbs

with great care. The Preacher sought to find words of delight, and uprightly he wrote words of truth. (Eccl. 12:9–10)

That process is especially true for wisdom and poetic literature, as we will see, but it also might generally describe all the writing of the Bible. We have glimpsed the way the biblical books hold together and reward close examination of their words and shapes and central themes. God by his Spirit carried along these authors to write beautifully shaped and crafted books.

In fact, one way to explain what we mean by calling the Bible "literary" is to say that it consists of words carefully and imaginatively shaped into unified entities. Words used simply for informational purposes—such as when I tell my husband that I am going shopping—are not essentially literary words. But if I stop and comment that going shopping in the mall feels to me like a hunting expedition in a deep, dangerous forest, then my language is becoming more literary because I have shaped the information imaginatively. Different parts of the Bible evidence various levels and types of literary shaping, but each book is artfully and intentionally shaped by its writer(s)—every word weighed and arranged from beginning to end with great care. The whole Bible is in this sense a literary work.

Implications

Reading for More than Propositions

How should this basic truth that the Bible is a literary work affect our expectations as we study its words? The first clear implication is that we should read the Bible for more than propositions. There will indeed be informational and factual propositions—propositional truth. But there will be more. What the writer of Ecclesiastes calls "words of truth" also include imaginative shaping of truth that we will be called to take in not just logically, as propositions, but also with our imaginations and our emotions . . . all of ourselves.

As I earlier noted the shape of Psalm 77, I was feeling again that psalmist's (and my own) experience of moving from despair to trust, from the oppressive "I cry" of the first verse to the beautiful "You led" of the final one. That poem does not state the proposition that a believer in despair can find hope through contemplating the works of God on behalf of his people. Rather, the poem imaginatively leads us through that experience and lets us understand it with our whole selves. In studying that poem, then, we should not jump immediately to a statement or an outline of its propositional truth. Rather, we should give ourselves to taking in the words and the lines and the sections one after another and all together.

"Studying the Word is life-changing; it is that which helps us know our Lord deeply and sweetly. It is the means he has chosen to reveal himself to us, and through which we can taste and see his goodness."

—Beth Wahl, Director of Women's Ministry, Front Range Alliance Church, Colorado Springs, Colorado

---

The recurring mention of Jesus' second coming in 1 Thessalonians should not just inform us of the book's main idea; that patterning of thought should also tug at our hearts, again and again, with the urgency of remembering this great trans-forming reality. Clearly, in studying any literary form we are accessing not just the form but the meaning of a text; form and content are always intertwined. The meaning of Psalm 77 and of 1 Thessalonians and of any unified literary text emerges through the form of the words.

We take in literature as more than just factual proposi-tions by opening ourselves not only to its imaginative shaping (form), but also to its imaginative word pictures (imagery). Let's return to Psalm 77 one more time and notice the picture there in verse 19, where the psalmist says to God:

> Your way was through the sea,
>   your path through the great waters;
>   yet your footprints were unseen.

In this allusion to the miracle of the Red Sea's parting, the psalmist imagines and pictures God as striding along ahead of the people, his feet perhaps accomplishing the parting of the waters with each step—even though the people couldn't see him or his footprints. He was there, doing it! Rather than just stating that God himself parted the Red Sea, and that God is powerful, and that God intervenes to save his people, the psalmist offers a vivid picture of God's huge, powerful pres-ence working that grand miracle.

I mention imagery at this point because, although imagery especially characterizes poetry, imagery appears in any and every genre of literature. Psalm 23 offers the metaphor: "The LORD is my shepherd." But the prophet Ezekiel also writes, "For thus says the Lord GOD: 'Behold, I, I myself will search for my sheep and will seek them out'" (Ezek. 34:11). In the Gospels, Jesus is quoted as saying, "I am the good shepherd"

(John 10:14). And Peter in his first epistle writes, "For you were straying like sheep, but have now returned to the Shepherd and Overseer of your souls" (1 Peter 2:25). Such imagery throughout Scripture speaks to us not just in propositions, but in pictures that feed our imaginations and our souls with the truth of God. The truth of this shepherd/sheep language—the truth that God rescues us and cares for us—can be stated propositionally, but it can be communicated imaginatively and emotively through imagery, story, and other literary means.

Imagery in particular accomplishes what literature by its nature accomplishes: it brings truth into concrete reality so that we can connect with it personally and experientially. I can logically grasp that God rescues and cares for me, but I can smell the sheep and feel their wool. The huge concrete impact of imagery throughout Scripture came home to me more fully when I had the privilege of working as one of the many contributors to the *Dictionary of Biblical Imagery*. I recommend this resource as one helpful way to connect such images throughout Scripture and to relish and grasp their full scriptural meanings.[3]

Reading the Bible for more than propositions means that we relish its beauty more and more, as that very beauty leads us more fully to grasp the truth. Some, indeed, have been slow to allow enjoyment of the Bible's literary beauty along with understanding of its theological truth. Literary critic Robert Alter writes:

> For many readers, it has been something of an embarrassment that there should be literature in the Bible, or that the Bible should ever be thought of as literature. If it is revealed truth, if it is meant as a guide to the moral life and a source of theological principle, if it is the authoritative account of

the first and last things, what, after all, does it have to do with literature? Let me hasten to say that one does not have to be a Bible Belt fundamentalist to entertain such views. T. S. Eliot, in the years after his conversion to Anglicanism, several times publicly reproved those who read the Bible for its poetry instead of for its religious truth.[4]

Let's just ignore the swing at "Bible Belt fundamentalists" and admit that sometimes this blindness to the Bible's literature has existed—on many fronts.

Our response should not be defensiveness, but rather delight with abandon in the beautiful literature of the Bible. Of course, we could call up one of our greatest defenders, C. S. Lewis. He perhaps says it best:

> What must be said, however, is that the Psalms are poems, and poems intended to be sung: not doctrinal treatises nor even sermons. Those who talk of reading the Bible "as literature" sometimes mean, I think, reading it without attending to the main thing it is about; like reading Burke with no interest in politics, or reading the *Aeneid* with no interest in Rome. That seems to me to be nonsense. But there is a saner sense in which the Bible, since it is after all literature, cannot properly be read except as literature; and the different parts of it as the different sorts of literature they are.[5]

Relishing Literary Genres

Lewis's words lead directly to the second implication of the truth that the Bible is a literary work: we should relish its literary genres, which simply means its different kinds of writing. The two most general literary genres are prose and poetry. In general, prose is writing that exhibits a less concentrated form of literary characteristics like imagery, rhythm, and the shaping of ideas into compact lines. Poetry is writing that exhibits a more concentrated combination of such characteristics. Of course, some prose can be quite poetic, and some poetry can seem prosaic. And within these two big genres there are many smaller ones, such as prose narrative and prose epistles, or lyric poems and proverbs. One helpful way of applying genre study to the Bible is to consider Scripture's various sections as they relate in different and specific ways to these two main genres, prose and poetry.

Such an approach has been used profitably by many. For example, see the Appendix, in which David Helm of the Charles Simeon Trust helpfully offers what he calls genre-specific questions for the study of Scripture. The seven questions suggested in chapter 4 do work for any genre, I believe, but it is true that the more carefully we consider those questions, the more they lead into genre-specific considerations.

Gordon D. Fee and Douglas Stuart organize their whole book *How to Read the Bible for All Its Worth* around specific ways to approach the different biblical genres.[6] Whether we start with this genre approach or incorporate it naturally into our study, we must learn to observe and respond to the distinct types of literature God inspired. Dealing with genres opens the text, as we learn to look for different elements that characterize different genres. Such attention to genre in the end lets us worship more profoundly the Creator and source of all beauty, as we take in the amazing diversity of literary forms inspired by the one who spoke words to create the diversity of stars and seas and animals and nature and human beings.

I will briefly discuss both prose and poetry in relation to the outlined sections of Scripture below. Many more complex divisions can be drawn and more specific comments made, but let's start here. We'll discuss prose in the remaining part of this chapter, and we'll relish the subject of poetry in the next.

Prose
    1. Narrative
        a. Old Testament
        b. Gospels and Acts
    2. Epistles
Poetry
    3. Wisdom Literature and Psalms
Prose and Poetry Together
    4. Prophetic and Apocalyptic Literature

Prose

Narrative: Old Testament

The first more specific literary genre we meet in Scripture, starting with Genesis, is a form of prose called *narrative*, which simply means the writer is telling a story. Scripture's narrative mode (with the exception of stories like the parables) is historical rather than fictional, as it is telling a true story, one that really happened. Old Testament narrative begins in Genesis and moves (with some interruptions) through Esther, also reaching into portions of the prophetic literature.

Narrative usually works on more than one level. Ruth, for example, is the story of one woman and one family. But it is also one episode in the whole Bible's story of God's redeeming a people for himself through Jesus Christ his Son. We will get to the level of the whole-biblical story (often called the meta-narrative), and our discussion of the Bible's story will not be complete until then. Actually, however, careful treatment of Scripture's individual narratives leads to fuller understanding of the metanarrative.

"I have learned that Old Testament is actually an easier genre than the Pauline literature to understand. The early narratives are a great and crucial place for beginners to start. . . . Non-Christians often need to read lots of the Bible before they become Christians. They cope with the Old Testament just fine, and this sets them up for success with the New Testament."

—Bron Short, Bible study leader and writer, St. John's Shaughnessy, Vancouver, British Columbia, Canada

---

Three commonly acknowledged elements of narrative that we should take care to notice include *character, action,* and *setting.* We have touched on the general question of *characters,* but it is important to reemphasize their importance as basic to propelling a narrative along its way. The narrator is perhaps the first character to note—in the Bible one who less often stops to comment on the story and more often shows and tells through his narrative tools. He takes us into scene after scene where we watch the characters—and hear them speak. The characters' dialogue becomes an indispensable tool used by the narrator to shape and develop the story. It is dialogue—those spoken words rather than extensive physical description or moral commentary—that often lets us know who the characters are and what they're like.

After a short introduction to the story of Ruth, what comes first in the text? What comes first is dialogue, a conversation between Naomi and her two daughters-in-law—a conversation that not only sets up the action of the story but also reveals the women's hearts. We receive no physical descriptions or commentary on their actions, but from their words we learn that Naomi is a bitter, empty woman who blames God, and Ruth is a woman of courage and loyalty who embraces God. Ruth's often-quoted words right at the heart of the first chapter (Ruth 1:16–17) not only are beautiful but also reveal her wholehearted commitment to God and his people. The first verse of chapter 2 does bring a short introductory description of Boaz as a "worthy man," but it is his words and his actions that let us see his worthiness, in his interaction with his workers and especially in his interaction with Ruth. Our imaginations love to picture a handsome, virile man and a lovely young woman—as they may well have been—but in the text it is the dialogue that introduces them to us.

What the characters' dialogue advances is the *action*, the plot. In Old Testament narrative especially, the plot is the thing. By *plot* we mean the way the story develops from the beginning, through the middle, to the end. The basic narrative plot shape is often described as an initial introduction of conflict that builds to some kind of resolution. This short description explains the shape of a great many biblical stories and the shape of the one big biblical story as well. Or perhaps we should say that the shape of the one huge, true story of the universe explains all the other stories that could ever be told. In any case, think of what happens in Eden for an early example of narrative plot shape. Conflict is introduced, discord builds, and a sad resolution is reached—although with a hint of a good resolution to come; the Eden story is perfectly set up for a sequel.

Ruth offers a helpful example in its short, compact narrative (like Esther). In this story conflict is introduced immediately both on a larger level with the famine in Bethlehem and on a more personal level with the deaths of all the men in Naomi's family. Resolution appears, grows, and finds its climax through Boaz the kinsman-redeemer and his union with Ruth. The basic plot shape is certainly evident.

But what we should notice further is how intricately the biblical narrative plot is shaped, with carefully arranged patterns. We mentioned Ruth's beautiful initial words. What is beautiful about them is their poetic patterning. We sense the joining, the heart's overlay of "where you go" with "I will go," and "where you lodge" with "I will lodge," and "your people" with "my people"—and, as the climax and the point, "your God" with "my God." That sort of symmetrical patterning is one chief and noticeable characteristic of Hebrew literature, and it extends from the level of words to the level of the whole narrative.

Consider the patterning of the narrative of Ruth—which is not just the love story of Ruth and Boaz. Their story is encased in the story of Naomi, with whom the whole narrative begins and ends. Sometimes this method of encasing is called an *inclusio*, which in this case leads us to see the larger story of Naomi, who begins empty (see Ruth 1:21) and who ends full, with her offspring filling her lap and all the women filling the air with praises to God the "restorer of life" (Ruth 4:14–16). The whole story is one of filling, moving from famine to rich harvesting, from death to life. Ruth the foreigner is the character who from the start reaches out her hands to seek the filling—first of God, and then of God through Boaz, from whom she asks and receives the provision of grain and the ultimate provision of a husband. Boaz celebrates the protective wings

70

of God as Ruth's refuge (2:12), and then in a mirroring passage Ruth seeks the protective wings of Boaz as her kinsman redeemer (3:9).

Examples abound in the book of Ruth, but the point is that the plot of this narrative is intricately patterned to show the main idea: the ways in which a God of covenant kindness fills our empty lives with his mercy. That's the main idea of this level of the story; we will have to go further. But to reach this level leads us well into the larger one.

Every biblical narrator has selectively chosen and arranged the action through a series of scenes and dialogues, with utmost care and patterning. The first two chapters of the Bible are some of the most highly patterned narratives in existence, with refrain-like repetitions of words and sequences. The highly patterned elements of Genesis do correspond with ancient literary practices, but in God's providence they also beautifully communicate the elaborate order and the beauty of creation.

The book of Esther represents one of the most elaborate works of art among all the biblical narratives, with its three feasts symmetrically marking its progress, its intricacies of plot turns, and its ironies of rising and falling characters crossing each other at just the right points. Such intricacy is surely explained not only by cultural convention; might we not say that God intended through such highly patterned narrative to point to the remarkable, moment-by-moment weaving of his providence, ultimately for the purpose of saving his people?

Along with the characters and action, we should notice *setting.* Bethlehem, the city of David, is mentioned—and left behind—right in the first verse of the book of Ruth. The action returns to Bethlehem, to the land of God's people, in order to find restoration from physical and spiritual famine and death. The warm domestic settings of home and harvest and birth within Bethlehem emphasize the richness of God's provision through families and generations of his people.[7] The setting of a story is important to note and often contributes to the meaning.

Looking ahead to the gospel narratives, we can see that movement toward Jerusalem shapes each one in general, with setting of the physical journey mirroring Jesus' own journey toward confrontation with those who do not believe—and toward the final confrontation of the cross itself. When we think of the Gospels, we might picture not only scenes on the road, on a mountainside, or in the temple; we might picture as well many scenes at a table, with food and drink and people gathered together around a meal. This intimate setting is important, as it mirrors the fellowship with himself that Jesus came to provide for us—perhaps pictured best by that final Passover meal in the upper room.

Narrative: Gospels and Acts

Although most of the comments so far concerning Old Testament narrative apply also to the Gospels and Acts, these New Testament books do operate somewhat distinctly. I would classify them as narrative because they tell the story of Jesus' life and the early church. In contrast to Old Testament narrative, the Gospels are organized much more centrally around teaching, which in each gospel fills up large portions of the text. That teaching is an integral part of the story these gospel writers are telling. If we started our reading in Genesis, we should not be surprised that Jesus finally comes as the Word and preaches words of powerful truth to the world.

The Gospels offer the most vivid evidence that biblical narrators select and shape material in order to create books with distinct themes and purposes. Even though each gospel offers true facts about Jesus' life, each writer sees and lets us see from a different perspective—so that those questions we ask become crucial: Who was each writer? When did he write his gospel, and for whom? What is the main idea? Each gospel needs to be studied on its own terms.

Luke was the only Gentile writer, a doctor who traveled with the apostle Paul and also wrote the book of Acts. Luke wanted to write "an orderly account" (Luke 1:3) that clearly documented the reach of the gospel to all, both Jews and Gentiles—an aim that was accomplished in both his books together. Matthew's gospel is more oriented to a Jewish audience, so that we might state his aim in terms of pointing to the promised Messiah, finally come to save. Mark, the earliest and most succinct, direct writer, orders his scenes into a compact whole that captures the rising conflict of Jesus the servant-king with a world that doesn't believe—a conflict climaxing in his sacrifice on the cross, alone. John's gospel, which was written later and stands apart from the much more in-common content of the three other "Synoptics" (the word literally means "common seeing"), seems more like an evangelistic work: John writes so that people who read will believe in the Christ and find life (John 20:31). Having said that each gospel should be studied independently, we should add that they also work together to tell a whole, full gospel story to the world.

Many whole books have been devoted to one distinct genre within the Gospels, that being the *parable*—those intriguing little stories that Jesus incorporated into his teaching. How should we study the parables? Probably not as separate entities. In general, parables are short, simple stories about everyday people. They are stories told with a purpose that we find in the context of the teaching where they appear. They are part of the teaching, teaching that must be either rejected or received. The parable of the sower is most helpful here and even might be said to be about the telling of parables. This parable (see Mark 4:1–20) is offered to a large crowd that doesn't understand it, but it is then explained by Jesus to a smaller group of followers who want to understand. The context illustrates the very meaning of the parable: the word is given to many people but received in a variety of ways. Jesus' interpretation, which attributes spiritual meaning to various details of the parable, shows that the parables are indeed meant to be interpreted for their symbolic meaning.

The sower of the seed in the parable, Jesus explains, represents the one who teaches the word. The seed sown on rocky ground represents the word that is received with joy but then abandoned in tribulation . . . and so forth. We should be careful not to spend all our time matching meanings (some details may not be symbolic), but rather to watch for the main meaning of the parable in its context and the ways its details communicate that meaning. The parable of the sower shows God's word (here, Jesus' teaching) as being rejected by many and received by a few; the point would be to condemn those who reject and to encourage Jesus' followers to listen and receive.

Epistles

Finally, prose, but not narrative prose, appears in the New Testament Epistles. The letters to the early groups of believers are just that: letters. The context of the writer and the audience to whom he writes are obviously important and are sometimes more clear than other times, but the fact that these are personal letters instead of theological treatises allows us to relate to them in a personal way—first by getting to know the early-church context and then finally by applying them to our own.

It is helpful to look for the basic epistle form, which includes first an opening greeting (often including a prayer); second, the body of the letter; and finally, a closing (often including personal details). Within this general form is packaged the powerful gospel teaching that presents the Lord Jesus Christ as the fulfillment of all the Scriptures and the salvation of the world, the one in whom and for whom we are called to live, until he comes again. We have noted Colossians' logical movement from theological teaching to practical application, and indeed that combination appears in most of the Epistles. Each epistle, however, has its own logical configuration and development that we should carefully observe and follow.

"Our Lord wants us to know him, to learn, to have our minds renewed, and to be transformed in the process. Studying his Word is a privilege we must not regard indifferently; it must be an intentional and concentrated practice."

—Beth Wahl, Director of Women's Ministry, Front Range Alliance Church, Colorado Springs, Colorado

---

The richness of the Bible's prose is overwhelming. Perhaps we tend to think of prose as less artful than poetry, but even this short glimpse into the masterful and varied shaping of scriptural prose should encourage us to study it as the treasure of literature it is. Our glimpse into poetry should do the same!

6

From Prose to Poetry . . .

More Literary Explorations

WE'RE IN THE MIDDLE OF DEVELOPING the implications
that grow from seeing the Bible as a literary work. As the first
implication, we talked about reading for more than propositions. Then we began to talk about relishing literary genres.
The two general genres of prose and poetry are both "literary"
because they both consist of artfully and imaginatively shaped
words that communicate truly but not just propositionally. In
general, we said, prose exhibits a less concentrated form of
literary characteristics like imagery, rhythm, and the shaping of
ideas into compact lines; poetry exhibits a more concentrated
combination of such characteristics. Having discussed biblical
prose, we're on to poetry!

First, it will be helpful to talk briefly about poetry, and
the Bible's poetry in general. What is all this poetry doing in
Scripture? Some books (Psalms, Song of Solomon, Proverbs,
and Lamentations) consist entirely of poetry. Others (like Job
and many of the Prophets) are mainly poetry. It helps to stand

back and notice that all this poetry does not serve primarily to advance the historical narrative of Scripture. The prose sections in general advance the action. The poetry sections serve mainly to speak in relation to the action.

Poetry often tends to be more emotive than prose: we might say that the Bible's poetry brings us cries from the hearts of God's people (as in Psalms) or from the heart of God to his people (as in the Pophets). The Wisdom Literature (Job, Proverbs, Ecclesiastes, and perhaps Song of Solomon) offers the poetic commentary (although sometimes in prose!) of wise men who stop along the way to ask questions about what's happening—sometimes more practical questions, as in Proverbs, and sometimes heavier questions, as in Job or Ecclesiastes.[1] All these are cries that open up the history and give it heart, color, emotion, and personal depth. The poetic voices are like a whole string of commentators standing on the sidelines of an exciting game and calling out concerning the action. Actually, they're more like people *in* the game who somehow have time to write about it as they play.

In Bible study groups, people often tell me that they just don't "get into" poetry; they'd rather study more straightforward texts. Several different responses would be possible on my part. One would be to say that a huge portion of the inspired Scriptures comes to us in poetry, and so we had better get into it. This actually is an important point, but saying it doesn't always help. Another possible response would be to point out that the more "straightforward" parts of Scripture aren't really any less complex than poetry to study—as we have seen even in a brief discussion of prose. In fact, prose may have a lot more complex meaning hiding in it than we tend to think, whereas poetry sort of flaunts its special ways of speaking and points attention to itself as poetry. There's a lot to look for, whether we're reading a story or a letter or a poem!

Another possible response is to say, "I understand. None of us really reads poetry regularly these days." Indeed, we are not a culture that generally gets into poetry! Gone are the days when people were in the habit of enjoying an evening of reading poems (or stories) out loud together. That habit carried much early literature through the stages of oral story-telling into the stages of written works. Homer's *Iliad* and *Odyssey* were for generations passed on by bards who recited the beloved stories aloud for various audiences. That was fun entertainment! The poetic elements of those epics made them especially easy to memorize—things like set epithets and epic similes and patterns of rhythm. (Poetry is in many ways much easier to memorize than prose.) Yes, I know this is not a lecture in literature. But it is important to see where we've come and *from* where we've come.

When I respond by saying I understand this problem with poetry, I usually add another comment, something to the effect that most of us do have sort of a natural instinct for poetry. We all habitually use one of poetry's most distinguishing elements, picture-language—even in cliché statements like "I'm at the end of my rope!" We enjoy the rhythm of song, the texts of which are often poetry. We read poetry to children and find in them a natural enjoyment of the rhythm and rhyme and fun of playing with words. How many of us still recall the pleasure of chanting by memory lines like those of Robert Louis Stevenson:

How do you like to go up in a swing,
    Up in the air so blue?
Oh, I do think it the pleasantest thing
    Ever a child can do!

Many of us tend to squash that instinctive love for poetry rather too quickly in children as they grow.

That instinct, however, is never completely squashed. It is fascinating to observe how people use poems to try to express their feelings in times of deep emotion. The sense is that a simple propositional statement just won't capture the depths of experience. America's annual 9/11 commemoration ceremonies have regularly involved the reading of poetry, which evidently helps people express and process the grief and horror of that event. There are Web sites of poems commemorating that tragic day in 2001. Presidents have invited poets to recite poems for their inauguration ceremonies, in order to articulate the huge significance of these landmark national moments—from Robert Frost, who was invited by President Kennedy in 1961, to Elizabeth Alexander, who was invited by President Obama in 2009.

Public reading of poetry, though, is unusual these days, and private reading perhaps even more so. What we do instead has perhaps made the biggest difference in our interaction with literature. It is not my purpose here to talk about modern technology and television and the Internet; we are all aware of the both marvelous and harmful effects these relatively new developments have brought into people's lives and homes. The point is that many of us have lost our taste and our habit for one of the most natural and beautiful human activities instilled in us from creation.

It was Adam who spoke what might be called the first human poem. When God brought Eve to him, Adam said:

> This at last is bone of my bones
> > and flesh of my flesh;
> she shall be called Woman,
> > because she was taken out of Man. (Gen. 2:23)

Adam's response has to make us think about words, as we observe his first impulse to *name* Eve, his verbal play with the similar-sounding Hebrew words for "woman" and "man," and his celebration of the perfectly matched first husband and wife in these balancing, symmetrical units of meaning.

It is not surprising that much of the poetry still enjoyed or written today is love poetry, springing from that basic instinct to try to express, somehow, the depths of emotion experienced in the romantic connection with another human being. It all started with Adam. It all really started with God, the original word speaker. It all reflects the relational nature of the Trinity. The fact that all we sons and daughters of Adam and Eve are created in the image of God certainly connects to our own creations—and our poetic creations—with words.

So what about the poetry of the Bible? How should we study it? I would suggest first that we should quite openly and publicly enjoy it. We will have to spend time dealing with the specifics of it, some of which this chapter will address. But I have found it most helpful to approach poetry initially just by noticing it with joy and zest. Because poetic instincts are natural to us as human beings, this joy and zest can be contagious and can carry us into our study with an attitude of openness that we might not otherwise have.

I am often amazed that we can approach a text of poetry and forget even to notice that it is poetry, in our concern to get the propositional truth straight. How many of us have heard sermons on a psalm or a passage from Isaiah that do not take note of the fact that we're reading poetry? We can help not just by teaching the poetry as poetry when we get a chance, but also simply by relishing the poetry—taking delight in it—any chance we get!

A few years ago Dr. D. A. Carson visited us as the keynote speaker for a Reformation Lecture Series at Covenant College. His first talk offered a beautiful exposition of Psalm 1. But before he got to Psalm 1, he talked about Hebrew poetry. Before he got to Hebrew poetry, he talked about poetry. He talked about how wonderful poetry is and how we don't know that very well anymore. He talked about how he had been required in his childhood to memorize all kinds of poems; in fact, he stood up in front of the student body and recited by memory a Shakespeare sonnet, an E. E. Cummings poem, and a limerick. By the time he got to Psalm 1, we were all noticing—and enjoying—the fact that this was poetry!

"How can you describe a sunset to a blind person in a way that makes that person want to see it and delight in it? I don't have a clue. But if we surround someone with the sunset and by God's grace he opens their eyes, I'm convinced that will only be the beginning of his or her desire to see more of the wonder of his creation. If this is true of his creation, shouldn't the wonder of God's person, as revealed to us in his Word, be a hundred times more compelling?"

—Teren Sechrist, Bible study teacher, Berean Baptist Church, Livonia, Michigan

---

Approaching the biblical poetry a bit closer in, we see that it comes in different kinds of packages. Many of the questions we will ask apply no matter what package the poetry comes in. But it helps to notice the packages, which for our purposes we will divide into three kinds: (1) the *lyric poem*; (2) the *proverb*; (3) the *longer poetic passages.*

1. A lyric poem is a self-contained, generally short, and often emotive expression—as in all the psalms.
2. A proverb is an even shorter, more compact, memorable poetic statement; these come in concentrated form in the Wisdom Literature but also appear scattered throughout the Old and New Testaments.
3. The longer poetic passages can be narrative poetry, as in Job, or long prophetic messages, as in some of the Prophets like Isaiah.

Whatever the package, biblical poetry has specific characteristics that will help us "get into" it. Let's talk first about the *form* and second about the *imagery* of biblical poetry.

The Form of Biblical Poetry

We talked about form in general when we discussed the questions of crux and context and configuration, and we used those questions profitably in relation to Psalm 77. But we did not talk about the way Psalm 77 (and all biblical poetry) comes to us in paired units of thought—mostly two, sometimes three or more units balancing together in what we should see, in our English translations, as pairs of lines on the page. This chief characteristic of Hebrew poetry is called "parallelism," which simply refers to the balancing together of units of thought, mostly in pairs.

Anytime we study biblical poetry, we should stop to celebrate God's providence in making this aspect of his Word accessible to people who read it in all different languages. C. S. Lewis makes this point well, as he discusses parallelism:

"It is (according to one's point of view) either a wonderful piece of luck or a wise provision of God's, that poetry which was to be turned into all languages should have as its chief formal characteristic one that does not disappear (as mere metre does) in translation."[2] Without reading in the Hebrew, we cannot hear the beautiful rhythms and cadences of the original poetry. But how amazing that we *can* actually begin to understand and even feel the rhythm of the thoughts as they come one and then the next, like one wave and then another on the shore, in that matching symmetry that we begin to recognize as this poetry's most basic shape.

Many books offer instruction concerning the various kinds of parallelism in Hebrew poetry. Lee Ryken offers helpful and detailed discussion of biblical poetry in his *Words of Delight*. It is important for us to be able to recognize at least three generally acknowledged types of parallelism:

1. Synonymous parallelism, in which the second line repeats in some way the meaning of the first;
2. Antithetical parallelism, in which the second line contrasts with the first;
3. Synthetic parallelism, in which the second line completes in some way the meaning of the first.

Attention to these kinds of parallelism is not simply a technical matter but often contributes to the understanding of a text. A good group leader or member of a Bible study will always want to stop and ask, "What's the point"—for example, of noticing an instance of synonymous parallelism. Let me comment briefly on the point of noticing such technicalities.

Synonymous parallelism involves repetition, but the second line is never exactly the same as the first. Often the meaning will simply be expanded by a parallel word or phrase that gets at the same meaning but adds a different aspect to it. If we don't notice the parallel relationship of the words, then we won't put them together to create the meaning; we may even take them as two completely different ideas, one after the other. The form of this poetry tells us that it works through relationships in meaning. That in itself is a compelling concept, from a theological point of view. In literature, form and content always go together.

I recall a recent group discussion in which we were trying to define meditation on Scripture. Psalm 1:2 was the source of our discussion:

> But his delight is in the law of the LORD,
> and on his law he meditates day and night.

Lots of people in this group had good ideas about what it means to meditate on Scripture. But we really made progress when one person in the group noticed the parallel lines of verse 2 and put together *meditating* on the law with *delighting* in the law. Meditating on God's Word involves not just a deep examination but also, in the very process, a delighted tasting and savoring of its meaning as it unfolds. It might be possible to classify this verse as synthetic rather than synonymous parallelism and to say that line 2 simply continues the idea. Even so, we would have to connect delight with the logical outcome or manifestation of meditation: there is a relationship between the two. That relationship helps unfold the full meaning of what the psalm is telling us to do with the law. Of course, the context of the verses around this verse expand on the meaning, with the contrast of what the blessed man *doesn't* do in verse 1 and the picture of what his blessedness looks like in verse 3.

Antithetical parallelism appears in Psalm 1:6, the psalm's last verse, where the way of the righteous is contrasted with the way of the wicked—the culmination of a contrast that grows all the way through the psalm:

> For the LORD knows the way of the righteous,
>> but the way of the wicked will perish.

Actually, the easiest place to find this kind of parallelism is Proverbs, which is all about contrasting the way of the wise with the way of the fool. But Psalm 1, sometimes thought of as the gateway into the psalms, starts out by setting forth these two opposite ways and calling us into the one that leads to life, the one where we will find all these heart cries of God's people to meditate on and be encouraged by.

This first psalm's final contrast is telling in its variation. Two different *ways* are contrasted, but there's not an exact match in the other parts of the statements: we find neither two different masters (the LORD and ?) nor two different destinations (? and perishing) in these parallel lines. The master who knows one way is contrasted with the destination of the other way. We might say that the destination of the righteous is only and all about the LORD (*Yahweh*, the covenant name for God) who personally knows and watches over his own to the end. And that LORD has no parallel; without him there is only perishing.

Parallelism, then, is the most basic formal structure we encounter when we read any of the Bible's poetry. This structure should neither scare us away nor bore us. Perhaps we should imagine that the two parallel units of thought reach toward each other and make a doorway through which we can pass. That thought leads us to the next characteristic of Hebrew poetry: its imagery.

The Imagery of Biblical Poetry

The term *imagery* simply refers to language that images or pictures. Most poetry is full of imagery, and Hebrew poetry is no exception; in fact, its images are especially vivid and rich. Pictures work on many levels, starting with the simple level of a description rich in sensory detail—a verbal picture that comes to life in our imagination. The tree in Psalm 1:3 is a famous example: we picture the streams of water next to it, the fruit it bears, leaves that are full and green, not withered. Sights, sounds, colors, perhaps even tactile sensations fill out this picture and make it rich to contemplate.

But imagery often does more: it often uses such a picture for the sake of some kind of comparison, so that one thing is pictured in terms of another. We noted earlier the thread of Scripture's comparisons of the Lord to a shepherd. Of course, in Psalm 1 it is the blessed man introduced in verses 1–2 who is like the tree in verse 3. This simile (comparison using *like* or *as*) reveals the nature of this man's blessedness through the picture. We can never summarize all that a picture means, but as we meditate on it (and delight in it!), the meaning grows. Planted stability (being rooted in the Word?) . . . multiple streams of water that (like the Word?) cleanse, refresh, satisfy, relax . . . fruit and green leaves (the good works that evidence a heart full of the Word?). . . the meaning of a picture grows richer and richer as we take time to muse on it.

I've seen some of the best Bible study small-group discussions happen on those occasions when a leader stops to encourage a group to muse together on a picture—first taking time to see the picture itself in as much vivid sensory detail as possible according to the details of the text, and then taking time to think together on the nature of the comparison being drawn. This is a much different process from just looking for one quick answer. It takes time to look at a picture. You can't neatly summarize it and go on or you'll miss it. We can learn much from each other as we take time to see together into the imagery of Scripture's poetry.

"Our Bible study group has been studying the psalms, the magnificent poems of a shepherd/king directed to his heavenly Father many centuries ago. How amazing that those same words are touching the lives of people now—people of all ages and in all the various situations and crises of our modern world. Truly, the Word of God is living and powerful, sharper than any two-edged sword."

—Wendy Williams, Bible study leader, Lookout Mountain
Presbyterian Church, Lookout Mountain, Tennessee

Psalm 1:3 (trying to contain that tree) is a solid, fat, full verse, with even an extra line at the end to cap it off. By contrast, the next verse quickly blows by, just like the chaff it pictures in that simile of the second line. The wicked have no roots or solidarity to make them strong and lasting like the righteous. The ongoing contrast emphasized by these pictures is even more dramatic when we notice that one single man is being contrasted with the wicked, plural. The righteous man stands out. He is solid and alive, like that tree. The indistinct crowd of wicked people cannot stand but are just blown away.

What is this poem, Psalm 1, about? Perhaps it is about the contrast between the righteous and the wicked. Or perhaps it is about the blessing of the one who loves God's Word, in contrast to the many who don't. We've noticed only part of the imagery in this poem, but we've seen how integral the imagery is to the poem's meaning.

Imagery works through all kinds of comparisons: simile, metaphor, personification, and even metonymy and synecdoche. Those last two words are simply fun to say! We can look up such terms and many more, but the principle is that poetry constantly pictures one thing in terms of another. As a result, poetry on the level of its pictures is not literally true. A man who delights in God's law does not have leaves growing on him. And there is no special piece of furniture for scoffers, no actual seat where that man does not sit.

Even in the prose of the New Testament Epistles, the imagery creates a nonliteral level, so that Paul in Colossians 2:6 is not talking about how we actually walk along with our two feet. In Colossians 3 he is not talking about material clothes we take off and put on. These are, of course, comparisons: walking is like making spiritual progress, and putting off clothes is like rejecting sinful practices, and so forth. These concrete pictures help us take in the meaning through our imaginations.

The Bible is true, but because of its literary aspects, especially its imagery, it is not always literal. Only by careful study of the context of each verse and passage and book can we discern what imagery might be at work and what the writer is trying to communicate. We can see that it is of utmost importance to become sensitive to Scripture's imagery and how it works. It is of utmost importance to become sensitive to the whole scope of Scripture's literary aspects so that we will learn to receive what God intended through these masterful writers of his inspired and inerrant Word. God could have inspired an outline or a list of truths. Instead, he inspired a literary work. Kevin Vanhoozer suggests that we actually redefine *literal*, so that "the literal sense is the sense of a literary act." He explains:

> Taking the Bible literally means reading for its literary sense, the sense of its communicative act. This entails, first, doing justice to the propositional, poetic, and purposive aspects of each text as a communicative act and, second, relating these to the Bible considered as a unified divine communicative act: the Word of God.[3]

The more we learn to read "literarily," the more we will be opening our ears to hear God's Word.

I have discussed the poetic characteristics of form and imagery in relation to one lyric poem, Psalm 1, but these same characteristics will be present and will contribute to the meaning of whatever poetic "package" we're studying. These "packages" are varied and complex, as we've seen and as we will note in some final comments on biblical literature in which poetry and prose combine.

Final Comments on Prophetic and Apocalyptic Literature

Both Old Testament prophetic literature and the New Testament book of Revelation contain poetry *and* prose, and both reach out in layers of time to the end of human history. However, these final two categories are quite distinct, with the Old Testament prophets speaking into events surrounding the exile, and Revelation speaking into the church in the last days.

The Old Testament prophets, from Isaiah through Malachi in our English Bible, were speaking into history more than writing it (although some sections are narrative). Prophecy can be classified as a special genre all its own, one we might describe as "declaration." The Old Testament prophets' job was to declare the word of the Lord; God spoke to them, and they brought that word to the people. Jeremiah describes himself as one "to whom the word of the LORD came" (Jer. 1:2); Amos opens his book crying out, "The LORD roars from Zion and utters his voice from Jerusalem" (Amos 1:2); Micah's prophecy is introduced with these words: "The word of the LORD that came to Micah of Moresheth" (Mic. 1:1).

Of course, others besides these "writing prophets" prophesied throughout the Old Testament. Moses, for example, was the great prophet through whom God spoke his law, and the prophets Elijah and Elisha spoke God's word into the earlier years of the kingdom. But from the eighth through the sixth century B.C., prophets such as Isaiah began writing down their prophecies. Those who wrote longer books are designated "major prophets," and those who wrote shorter books "minor prophets."

Those three centuries spanned the period during which the northern and southern kingdoms of Israel and Judah dramatically declined, were conquered, were driven into exile, and then returned as a remnant to their land. That history and the biblical books covering that history must be clear in order to understand the voices of the prophets who speak God's word into that history. Amos and Hosea (and Jonah) came first in the decades before the fall of the northern kingdom to Assyria in 722 B.C. Isaiah prophesied through the time of that fall and after, anticipating the next fall—of the southern kingdom of Judah to Babylonia in 586 B.C. Micah and Jeremiah also prophesied in the years leading up to the fall and exile of Judah; Ezekiel and Daniel prophesied during that exile; Haggai, Zechariah, and Malachi are the "postexilic" prophets who speak into the time of the return of the remnant to Jerusalem.

I have not mentioned all the prophets, but even these examples show the way the prophets find their places in clusters around key historical events. One of the most important starting points in reading prophetic literature is getting the historical context straight so that we can have an idea of how these words resounded when the original speaker declared them to his original audience. There's also great satisfaction in getting the feel of the main contours of biblical history and arranging these prophets in their places as part of the whole story.

There's also a much greater possibility of developing appropriate conclusions and applications when we have understood the prophets in their original context. It is easy to swoop up many of their strong, beautiful cries and to import them directly into our own worlds—where they must come, but surely not without first being firmly grounded in their own place and time. Isaiah 37:26 is a remarkable verse, which begins:

> Have you not heard
>> that I determined it long ago?
> I planned from days of old
>> what now I bring to pass.

Isaiah 37:28 is beautiful, too (and reminiscent of Psalm 139):

> I know your sitting down
>> and your going out and coming in.

It is true that these verses, or parts of verses, present general truths about God's sovereignty and omniscience, truths that we might want to extract and apply immediately to our own situations.

"People often think their questions of the text and God are more important than God's questions of them; this has to be dealt with. People think they themselves are located at the center of interest in the text; they need to find God there, instead. This is a revolution that has to happen at some stage in all readers of Scripture."

—Bron Short, Bible study leader and writer, St. John's Shaughnessy, Vancouver, British Columbia, Canada

---

These words from Isaiah 37, however, come to us as part of an amazing oracle of God brought by the prophet Isaiah to King Hezekiah, in response to Hezekiah's prayer of supplication for God's help in dealing with evil King Sennacherib of Assyria, whose army is at his gates. God answers Hezekiah by letting him hear this oracle about King Sennacherib, in which Sennacherib's doom is declared. That God should answer this way, by letting Hezekiah overhear his divine declaration against the enemy, is itself fascinating. The first layer of application perhaps should concern our understanding of God's response to one who shakes his fist at God and at God's people—as well as God's response to the earnest prayers of his people. The next layer probably should have to do with our view of and our response to ungodly political leaders who think they're in charge and have no idea that they are part of the sovereign plan of the one true God. The layer of simple personal application is there, but it's definitely not the first one, and it will be affected by the layers that come first.

Identifying not just context but also major themes is important in studying prophetic literature. Into the events surrounding the exile the prophets spoke words with recurring themes, themes of both judgment and salvation. Abraham's descendants had been called to be God's people and to follow the law given through Moses. The prophets' consistent message was that the people were not acting as God's people and they were not obeying his law. And so the prophets' words brought condemnation of the people's disobedience, warning of God's judgment on disobedience, and a call to renewed obedience.

These descendants of Abraham had also been given promises, covenants from God. The prophets brought words of hope as they reminded the people of these promises and called them to love and follow God in light of them. The prophets' call for obedience was at its heart a call for God's people to live by faith in God's promises so that the fruit of those promises might take root in their hearts and lives.

Readers feel the rhythm, or perhaps the tension, of judgment warnings and salvation promises in the prophetic literature. We also feel the rhythm of near and far: the warnings and the promises reach into close-up events like the Babylonian exile and the promised return from exile, but they also reach out farther to the ultimate judgment and hope to come at the end of human history. The Prophets, situated as they are at the end of the Old Testament, provide a crucial link between the revelation of God's covenant promises and the fulfillment of them in Jesus Christ.

In general, what literary style should we look for in the poetry and prose that fill the prophetic books? It's a preaching style, a style characterized by the passion of a Spirit-filled preacher and by the variety that would be represented by the whole lot of preachers alive even today, or throughout the past few centuries. There is a shape to each book, just as every great sermon has a carefully designed shape.

A huge, intimidating prophecy like Isaiah's unfolds beautifully to us when we learn the historical context, look for the main themes, and examine how the book unfolds those themes. My study of Isaiah was revolutionized by seeing its central two-part story of Judah's King Hezekiah (Isa. 36–39) as the book's hinge or bridge, connecting on this side to kings and nations in the context of Assyria's threat, and connecting on the far side to other kings and nations in the context of Babylonia's threat. On both sides many little sinful kings are judged in relation to the one King of heaven, whom Isaiah sees sitting on that throne at the start.[4] It is that King who brings about the victory and salvation promised in the end for all the nations, after the suffering of the exile has ended, finally and completely. That promise of salvation, starting in Judah and reaching all the nations, holds the book together from beginning to end. Isaiah is mostly poetry, and its exalted poetry matches the breadth of its vision.

The book of Revelation might be called New Testament prophecy; it is clear at the start that John is communicating a direct message from God: "The revelation of Jesus Christ, which God gave him to show to his servants the things that must soon take place" (Rev. 1:1). Revelation's particular kind of prophecy is called "apocalyptic," which according to its Greek root means "revelation." Apocalyptic literature *reveals* invisible realities both present and future, and it does that often through the use of highly symbolic elements. Parts of Old Testament prophecies as well might be called apocalyptic, particularly in the books of Ezekiel, Daniel, and Zechariah.

Apocalyptic literature brings us perhaps the most seemingly fantastical imagery of the Bible—imagery picturing not
just the world as we know it, but also worlds we do not know
or see with our physical eyes. None of us has ever seen what
Ezekiel describes: those four living creatures each with four
faces (of a human, a lion, an ox, and an eagle) and four wings,
moving around connected to those gleaming wheels within
wheels, under an expanse of shining crystal, with a throne of
sapphire above, upon which is seated a brilliant, fiery figure
with a human appearance (Ezek. 1). None of us has ever seen
a figure like the one John describes standing among seven
golden lampstands, clothed with a long robe and a golden
sash, with hair like white wool, like snow, eyes like a flame of
fire, feet like burnished bronze, a voice like the roar of many
waters, a mouth from which comes a sharp two-edged sword, and
a face shining like the sun in full strength (Rev. 1:12–16).

It does make sense that writers inspired to reach out to
worlds as yet unknown should be inspired with images unlike
anything we know. Such pictures should jolt us and humble us
before the huge invisible present and future realities to which
we are often totally oblivious. However, such pictures can also
involve difficulties of meaning. As we don't always know or
understand the literal reality that is being pictured, we don't
always know how to distinguish the literal from the nonliteral. In
this case, questions like those suggested in the Appendix become
most helpful, relating not only to the specific contexts of each
book, but in large part to the whole big story of the Scripture,
centered in Jesus, and the role these books play in that story.

How does a text relate to the gospel story? How does a text
anticipate or recall the death, resurrection, and reign of Jesus
Christ? We must now give direct attention to the truth that the
Bible is one whole story with Jesus Christ at the center.

If the Bible Is One Whole Story . . .

Then How Should We Read It?

Truth №5: The Bible is one story.

Implications for study:

1. Asking the question: Where is Christ in this passage?
2. Using Scripture to interpret Scripture
3. Enlarging perspectives

The Bible Is One Story

It is possible that this chapter and this truth about Scripture should have come first. I thought it should come either first or last. Let me tell you why I'm glad it's last. First of all, we've been referring to it all along, directly and indirectly, so that we already have a sense of how integral this truth is to everything we do in Bible study. The truths and implications discussed in this book do have a logical order, but they all need to work together simultaneously in the end. The ongoing process of study involving all these truths and implications cannot be an inflexible series of steps. The process is more organic than that, with a flexible and full-bodied approach centered in the Word itself and what it is. Many different books and texts within Scripture will call us more or less quickly to different implications of these truths, perhaps in different orders. This last truth is the largest overlay, which continually colors and unifies all the others. This last truth—of the unified story of the Bible—has to be in place.

Before proceeding, I want to acknowledge how much I have been helped in thinking about this truth not only by local church training but also by several key books, books that unpack this subject of biblical theology with formal expertise and detailed attention to the biblical text. Writers like Graeme Goldsworthy, Edmund Clowney, and more recently Vaughan Roberts beautifully celebrate the Bible as one unified work.[1] Such writers balance a fundamental respect for Scripture's doctrinal and propositional truths with a great sensitivity to the way Scripture unfolds these truths from beginning to end.

Literary perspectives can help in getting at this subject; after all, we're talking about *story*, which is narrative. Not every section of the Bible is narrative, but the Bible as a whole advances one overarching or *meta*narrative. I will be somewhat and unashamedly "literary" in talking about the Bible's big story, leaning a bit on previous discussion of the Bible as a literary book. In fact, many of our previous discussions converge and lead us logically toward this climax of seeing the Scriptures as a unified narrative. If God is the one narrator who breathed out all these words, then it makes sense that these words hold together in one book—even though this book is made up of sixty-six different little books, written by about forty different human authors who spanned about sixteen centuries, used a great diversity of genres, and wrote in a couple of different main languages. Many people have tried to imagine the impossible task, from a human perspective, of getting all these different writers "on the same page" through some workable literary action plan. Only the ultimate narrative perspective— the fact that this book is actually God speaking through different human authors—can explain its amazing unity.

"We have used several Bible overview studies (a year and a half in length) that give people the sweep of the whole Scriptures. This radically transforms people's grip and then their confidence and capacity as readers."

—Bron Short, Bible study leader and writer, St. John's Shaughnessy, Vancouver, British Columbia, Canada

---

Understanding the smaller narratives and how they work will help us understand the larger, unifying one. For example, those three main elements of narrative—plot, character, and setting—are crucial not only to each narrative section and book but also to the whole big book. In thinking about the unifying plot of the Bible, I like to recall first the way in which a long, complicated novel can be effectively held together by a unified plot. In a really good novel the seeds for the whole story are there from the beginning, and when we finally get to the end we say, "Ah! I see how the author was heading here right from the start; it had to end just like this!"

Many people have read Jane Austen's *Pride and Prejudice* and have enjoyed that famous, sparkling first sentence: "It is a truth universally acknowledged, that a single man in possession of a good fortune, must be in want of a wife." In her witty, ironic tone, Austen sets forth the whole perspective with which the novel deals and which it will indeed overturn, as it is the nature of irony to do. With this one ironic statement she also introduces her reader to the central themes of marriage and money and society and all the issues at stake in the story of Elizabeth and Darcy and Jane and Mr. Bingley and all the rest of the cast of characters, so that when we finally reach the wonderfully happy ending, we feel we just had to arrive at the union of Elizabeth and Darcy. With their love these two main characters overturn the pride and prejudice we saw at work from the start both in them and in the society all around them. We said that a narrative involves the introduction of conflict and a movement toward resolution. In Jane Austen's novel, pride and prejudice are the source of the conflict introduced into this plot from the start, and the process of resolution involves overturning them.

Likewise, the Bible's beginning holds the seeds for the whole story to come. Even a brief look at its beginning and ending together makes this exceptionally clear. The very first sentence tells us that God created the heavens and the earth . . . and then in the final chapters we see "a new heaven and earth," as we hear God saying, "I am making all things new" (see Rev. 21:1–5). The Bible moves from creation to re-creation, in one grand inclusio. Setting plays its part, as the story moves from that initial paradise of Eden, where our first parents lived openly in God's presence, to the final paradise where, again, God will dwell with his people. All kinds of plot markers show us the continuity: in that first paradise we see the tree of life, front and center, "in the midst of the garden" (Gen. 2:9), and in the final paradise there is that tree of life again, "on either side," the text says, of the "river of the water of life" flowing from God's throne right "through the middle of the street of the city" (Rev. 22:1–2).

The fact that the leaves of this tree in the end are "for the healing of the nations" points to the fact that this huge plot, with its clear big bookends, involves conflict: the nations evidently become sick and need healing. The first heaven and earth are evidently destroyed, needing to be re-created. In fact, the first paradise is closed off with a curse, and not until the new one is opened up do we read those beautiful words, "No longer will there be anything accursed" (Rev. 22:3).

The story's conflict, we know, appears right away (in Gen. 3), with the serpent's introduction of evil into that perfect paradise and the curse that results. But we also know that the resolution of the conflict is promised, indeed in seed form, with God's words in Genesis 3:15 speaking to that serpent and referring to Eve. Even in the process of the curse comes the promise of the curse's resolution:

> I will put enmity between you and the woman,
>   and between your offspring and her offspring;
> he shall bruise your head,
>   and you shall bruise his heel.

The whole ensuing story of Scripture, leading up to the final resolution in Revelation 21–22, is the story of that

promised offspring (or seed) of the woman—who is anticipated, who comes, and who will come again. He is the one
who accomplishes the resolution of the conflict introduced
from the beginning.

Before we get to this main character of the biblical narrative, let's stop and take in the beauty of these "bookends"
of paradise that frame and unify the whole story. We notice
not only the narrative's symmetrical shape. We notice also
that the original plan of God will not be thwarted; it will
be accomplished in the end. God clearly planned from the
beginning for his created human beings to live in bodies,
on the earth, in full communion with him. With the early
introduction of the conflict, that early paradise disappears
so quickly, before we have time to peer as deeply into it as
we're drawn to do. It gets cut off, and that loss haunts us all
through the story. We're somehow homesick for that place
throughout the entire narrative, especially when the conflict
introduced by evil and sin so mars all the subsequent places
and people in the story.

But we are reminded again and again of that place of
perfect communion with God—through the Jerusalem temple, for example, with its Holy of Holies filled with God's
presence. We grieve when God's presence leaves the temple and when the temple is destroyed by the Babylonians;
we rejoice when the temple is rebuilt after the exile, even
though it is not as fine as before—because we're longing
along with the returned exiles for that lost place where God
dwells with his people.

We find that place only, finally, when Jesus the Word is
made flesh and dwells among us. He brings that lost place to
us, as he brings the very presence of God down to us in the
flesh and through his death brings us life in him. When we

put our faith in him, that place (in him) is our home, but according to Revelation we'll see it and know it fully in that new heaven and earth where the New Jerusalem comes to rest. It will be a city foursquare, shaped exactly in the same proportions as the temple's Holy of Holies, but needing no temple because "its temple is the Lord God the Almighty and the Lamb" (see Rev. 21:15–22).

How beautiful! The story holds together in Jesus from beginning to end. Through him is accomplished God's original plan for his created human beings to live in bodies (perfect, resurrected bodies), on the earth (a perfectly re-created earth), in full communion with him (communion restored completely and eternally by that promised seed). It's where the story has to end! It's paradise regained, but a new paradise with a Redeemer at the center.

We're already talking about the main character who unifies this plot as it moves along with such a huge host of characters and scenes. Indeed, it is he who holds all the action together from start to finish. It is true to say that the main character of Scripture is the Lord God himself, "the Alpha and the Omega . . . who is and who was and who is to come, the Almighty" (Rev. 1:8). God from whose breath all these words and all these characters emanate is the ultimate unifier of the plot. It is his story.

It is also right to focus on the second person of the Trinity, and to say that Jesus Christ the Son is the central character of the story God breathes out in Scripture. The Son is the Word who was with God and was God, there with God from the beginning (John 1:1–2). The Son is the one who entered the action of the human story, as this Word became flesh and dwelt among us (John 1:14). He is the one who is to come again in all his glory.

"I'm continually struck by 'the relevance of truth.' What may seem like an outdated, dry section of Scripture often becomes full of weight and beauty upon further study. As we approach God's Word and ask questions of the text, it's amazing how applicable it becomes. What does this passage tell me about who God is? Who I am? What does God require of me? What in life should be important to me? How does this address my fears, my hopes? Finally, *how does this point to Christ?*"

—Lisa Helm, Bible study leader and pastor's wife,
Holy Trinity Church, Chicago, Illinois

Jesus is the main "actor" in every part of the Bible's story: the one by whom all things were made in creation (John 1:3; Col. 1:16); the promised bruiser of Satan's head who was anticipated throughout the Old Testament; the one who finally did come in New Testament times to accomplish that bruising; and the one who appears again at the end to complete the denouement. Often in a narrative plot after the climax of the resolution there comes a "denouement," literally an "unraveling" of the story's strands—a conclusion that comprehensively works out every logical development of the climax. Scripture's climax, where the conflict is resolved, comes at the cross: the cross is the point where Jesus through his death and subsequent resurrection finally conquered the powers of evil, where God "disarmed the rulers and authorities and put them to open shame, by triumphing over them in him" (Col. 2:15). The climax of the cross has consequences, which are working themselves out in the "last days" in which we now live. This period of denouement will end with the consummation of the story, when Jesus comes again to live forever with his people in the new heaven and earth. Jesus holds the story together from the very beginning to the very end.

We are approaching the story of the Bible in a large and general sense, which probably needs to be done more often, before we delve into complicated outlines of its different sections—which also needs to be done and which can be found in the several books I have mentioned. I witnessed perhaps the most general and simple teaching along this line in a Sunday school class years ago, as we were teaching a group of young children the books of the Bible. The lead teacher used a kind of energetic chant that began with the question, "What does the Old Testament teach?" The children shouted back in unison, "Jesus is coming!" The teacher then shouted back to them, "What does the New Testament teach?" And the children shouted back, "Jesus has come!" That's it, in a nutshell!

Mark Dever also knows how to put it simply, even in introducing a very large and helpful book covering all the books of the Old Testament: "Indeed, Jesus Christ *is* the point of the Bible. It is all about him. If you wanted to sum up the Bible in one word, you could do so by pointing to Christ. The Old Testament makes promises about Christ, and the New Testament keeps promises in Christ."[2] That's about as simple and clear as it gets. However, if we wanted to formulate the main idea of the entire Bible a bit more in detail, how would we do it? There are many ways, but a good one will always keep Jesus at the center. Some speak of the Bible as the story of God establishing his kingdom through Jesus Christ the Redeemer-King. The summary I learned from my pastors years ago referred to the Bible as the story of God's redeeming a people for himself through Jesus Christ. Both of those good "nutshell" versions include God as the sovereign director, Jesus as the central actor, and a community of redeemed people belonging to God as the result.

This storyline unfolds in Scripture, as the story develops. Scripture offers not a revelation that changes in its different stages, but one that unfolds as all of God's promises point more and more clearly to Jesus Christ, who finally appears and fulfills them all. "All the promises of God find their Yes in him," Paul says (2 Cor. 1:20). The story of Scripture is the story of that truth being revealed more and more clearly—until, one day, every eye will see him.

This is the truth Jesus was teaching his disciples after the resurrection, when "beginning with Moses and all the Prophets, he interpreted to them in all the Scriptures the things concerning himself" (Luke 24:27). "All the Scriptures," Jesus says . . . "everything written about me in the Law of Moses and the Prophets and the Psalms must be fulfilled" (Luke 24:44). With this statement Jesus covers (and applies to himself) the entirety of the Old Testament, which in the Hebrew Bible was divided into three sections: the Law, the Prophets, and the Writings (which included the psalms. Jesus uses a part to refer to the whole: *synecdoche!*).

As Jesus taught his disciples how to understand all the Scriptures as the revelation of himself, I wonder where he started. Wouldn't we love to have been there—to hear the Creator speak of creation . . . the promised seed speaking of that promise of himself in Genesis 3:15 . . . the promised descendant of Abraham speaking of that covenant wherein God promised to bless all the nations of the world through Abraham's offspring (Gen. 12:1–3) . . . the promised Redeemer explaining how Moses redeemed the Israelites out of the slavery of Egypt, spared from death by the blood of that Passover lamb . . . the only one who perfectly fulfilled God's law speaking of God's gracious giving of the law to Moses . . . the final Prophet, the final Word from God, speaking about the promise of a prophet like Moses (Deut. 18:15–18) . . . the final Priest who offered the perfect sacrifice on the cross speaking about those Old Testament sin offerings (Heb. 7:23–28) . . . the eternal King speaking of God's promise to David of a descendant who will reign forever (1 Chron. 17:11–15). Seeing all the Scriptures in light of the promised Savior lights them up and makes them shine with the light of Jesus himself.

"When we've taken a gospel-centered, Christ-centered approach to Bible study and interpretation, people are more often 'transformed' rather than given merely a sense of obligation, with 'shoulds' and 'oughts' and 'musts.' As important as all that is, transformation of the heart and heart motivation is key; otherwise, we simply produce well-versed 'Pharisees,' and people grow weary of studying Scripture."

—Chuck Isaac, Pastor, Christ the King PCA, El Paso, Texas

We're already moving far into the territory of implications growing from this truth that the Bible is one whole story with Christ at the center. We can't talk about it without doing it! We should be "doing it" all the time in our Bible study groups. In the remainder of this chapter we will distinguish three (among many possible) implications, and then in the following chapter we will observe these implications at work, as we revisit some of the biblical books and passages already discussed in this book.

Three Implications

Asking the Question: Where Is Christ in This Passage?

The first implication is that we should ask that Question #5 (see chapter 4) that we did not discuss earlier: Where is Christ in this passage? How does this passage connect to the central character of all the Scriptures? Of course, the danger here is that we would not read and study the passage itself carefully, but rather jump too quickly to an interpretive grid that leads us to the Christological interpretation. That's another reason I like the order of these chapters. We have to read and observe and study the passage itself. As we do that, connections to Christ will emerge from the passage.

The moment we see the opening words of Psalm 22, we know that these words were fulfilled as Jesus spoke them on the cross. But knowing that does not mean we shouldn't start by analyzing the main idea and the shape of this psalm, a psalm of David, before we simply say it's about Jesus and are done with it. Actually, analyzing the psalm itself will unfold the shape of David's and ultimately of Jesus' suffering, as it moves down deep into the depths and then rises again back up to that final cry of "Finished!"

A related danger is that in our eagerness to see Christ in all of Scripture, we will impose on a text a meaning that isn't there. Some passages don't have such direct links to Christ. They all link up one way or another, but sometimes that way is more indirect than direct.

Psalm 77, for example, which we discussed in some detail, connects to Christ more indirectly through its celebration of redemption by God's own arm at the center of it, and its rehearsal of events like the exodus, where God indeed redeemed his people. There are words heavy with covenant

108

meaning, like *redeemed* and *steadfast love* (Hebrew *hesed*, which regularly in the Old Testament refers to God's covenant love for his people), and promises that will not fail. The reality of a covenant-making, redeeming God emerges in this psalm as the answer to despair, and we know these promises of redemption culminated in the perfect redemption accomplished by his Son. We have to get to Jesus, but this psalm is not about Jesus as directly as is Psalm 22. We should allow the connections to be more direct or less direct according to the text.

The Use of Scripture to Interpret Scripture

The second implication is that we should use Scripture to interpret Scripture—just as Martin Luther recommended. What we're doing is connecting all the parts of one big story, so that we can see the flow and the relationships among the parts. Psalm 22:1 ("My God, my God, why have you forsaken me?") is interpreted finally by Matthew 27:46.

In some New Testament passages, like Acts 2:22–32, we're fortunate enough to be able to observe the apostles (in this case Peter) showing us how to read the Old Testament in light of the New. Peter tells us clearly here, as he quotes Psalm 16 in his sermon, that David was looking ahead to Jesus' resurrection from the dead when he wrote that psalm. According to Peter, David actually "foresaw and spoke about the resurrection of the Christ, that he was not abandoned to Hades, nor did his flesh see corruption" (Acts 2:31). How generous of Scripture (how generous of God!) to offer such a concrete lesson in the use of Scripture to interpret Scripture.

The writer of Hebrews offers many examples of interpreting Old Testament passages in light of Jesus. The Gospels overflow with quotations of and references to Old Testament passages, as those writers show that Jesus is truly the Messiah promised throughout history. Scripture itself teaches us how one part of the story sheds light on another. The repeated caution is that only through careful observation and study of the text under consideration can we make the right connections. Turning to other parts of Scripture is not the one simple answer to a passage, but rather part of the process of studying it.

Enlarging Perspectives

Third, seeing the Bible's one big story should enlarge our perspectives not only on the Bible but also on everything else, including ourselves. Something happens to me when I am reminded that I am not the main character of the story I am reading. When I read the Bible as the big story of the whole universe, with Jesus at the center of it and myself as one little character who gets to participate in this story, then I am both humbled and encouraged.

"After asking 'What does it say?' and 'What does it mean?' and 'What does it matter?' the fourth question is: 'What does it add?' In other words, how does a passage move God's ongoing revelation along? Keeping this fourth question in mind helps us to remember that, yes, Bible study applies to me, but ultimately it uncovers God's ongoing plan. The ultimate goal of Bible study is learning what God is doing to fulfill his purpose and plan."

—Carol Ruvolo, author and Bible study leader, Heritage Christian Fellowship, Albuquerque, New Mexico

---

I am humbled because this is about so much more than me and because in the scope of things I have such a small part. I am not in charge. But I am encouraged because I see that the God in charge cares so deeply about my little part—that the big story in fact is made up of all sorts of little people whom he loves and redeems and uses in amazing ways. I am humbled because I see I'm part of the problem, the conflict in the story. But I am encouraged because the story's Author solved that conflict through his own Son. So I read the passages to learn first about him, and not just about me. And I encourage the group I am part of to aim for this larger perspective.

This enlarged perspective will affect our view of all the characters in the biblical narrative, and it will shape the ways we as readers identify with the characters. We will see every character in relation to Christ, and we will identify with a character or characters in relation to Christ. A common example is the story of David, who in the narrative of David and Goliath clearly points ahead to the anointed King and Conqueror to come in his line. What is our perspective as readers in relation to this character? With which character(s) in this story should we identify? Perhaps we should identify most fully with the people in that narrative who couldn't save themselves and who needed a deliverer to come and save them—an unlikely deliverer, a humble one. Perhaps our application will have to do with shouting praises in the streets for this conqueror, like the people in David's time did.[3]

When we see Christ in Psalm 22, we do not focus solely on our own suffering (or even David's suffering), which we find articulated in that psalm. We focus finally more on the suffering of Christ for us, the fact that he descended to utter separation from God so that we who deserve the suffering of that punishment do not have to experience it. Psalm 22 leads us in the end through suffering to deliverance, pointing ahead to Christ's resurrection and the results of that—all of which impels us to focus ultimately not on suffering but on letting nations and future generations know the good news of who Jesus is and what Jesus has done for us. The one big story is all about him.

> "Something that has fired the imagination and faith of folks in our church is to bring the literary and biblical-theological approach to the forefront. For instance, most would understand a familiar story like David and Goliath as an example of faith: in other words, 'Be like David.' This, of course, misses the point. The story is not about how a faithful person is to approach the giants in his or her life, but rather how the True King wages war. . . . If we could bring this focus to the laypeople's level and equip them to understand Scripture from the 'historical-redemptive' focus, it would be huge."
>
> —Chuck Isaac, Pastor, Christ the King PCA,
> El Paso, Texas

8

~~

Storyline Implications
at Work

THE TRUTH THAT THE BIBLE is one whole story with Jesus
at the center affects everything else—comprehensively and
beautifully. We've been incorporating the implications of this
truth in various ways throughout this book. Now, having introduced three specific implications in the last chapter, we will
transport these implications simultaneously to several places
in Scripture that we have already visited: Joshua, Ruth and
Esther, Psalms and Proverbs, and Isaiah.

In circling back and seeing these implications at work, we
focus primarily on Old Testament passages, as their connection to the main storyline of Christ is the one more in need
of further illumination. Publishers of study materials report
that New Testament studies sell in much higher quantities
than Old Testament studies. If we understood better the unified story of the two Testaments, we would better grasp their
equal importance as the Word of God in Christ.

Indeed, perhaps the most fundamental implication of all in
relation to Scripture's storyline, an implication implicit in all the
others, is that we must be always in the process of reading and

studying the full revelation of God, from Genesis to Revelation. The crucial context of the whole of Scripture is the point. How malnourished we will be if we just pick and choose sections—and how limited will be our grasp of the story God is telling. One certainly couldn't read a work of literature like *Pride and Prejudice* by simply selecting various passages; the storyline would crumble!

"While topical studies are valid, many folks use them for their soapbox issues. . . . For instance, the Bible is not primarily a book about Christian marriage and parenting; when that's the only angle from which a group studies Scripture, it begins to warp the balance of what the Bible says about Christian living as a whole. It actually is more beneficial to parenting to become a well-rounded disciple than it is to look for instructions about parenting in the Bible. Those things that make you a healthy disciple are what make you a good parent."

—Donna Dobbs, Director of Christian Education, First Presbyterian Church, Jackson, Mississippi

---

It is good to be reminded of the danger of approaching Scripture selectively, with one topic, or one interpretive framework in mind—whatever the nature of that topic or framework. Those who wish to study a "Green Bible," focusing on environmental issues, will miss other aspects of the story and be tempted to distort the aspects they treat in an effort to squeeze them into their interpretive mold. Those who wish to study with a special emphasis on women's issues—whether their perspective is egalitarian or complementarian—must take care not to focus on certain passages or themes while ignoring others. God has set before us a full table with a completely nourishing meal.

Implications at Work

Joshua

In previous discussion of Joshua, we said that this book's main idea concerns God's promised inheritance to his people. To see Joshua in light of the whole big story involves recognizing the pattern leading up to this point in Scripture, a pattern that shows how God works in the salvation of his people: in the *exodus* (in which we see redemption from slavery into the new identity of God's people); in the giving of the *law* (in which God's people are shown how to live as God's people); and in the inheritance of the *land* (in which God's people receive the rest and abundance God promised through Abraham). The pattern of God's working is clear and marvelous.

Part of the point of the Old Testament narrative is that this early acting out of the pattern is not sufficient; it is only an imperfect prefiguring of a perfect pattern and so cannot end the story with resolution and closure. The *exodus* is marked by the celebration of Passover, but then those blood sacrifices must be reenacted over and over again. The *law* is good but is not perfectly obeyed, as we see both throughout the books of Moses and in Joshua early on with that dramatic story of Achan's disobedience and the tragic results (chapter 7). The inheritance of the *land* is rich and abundant, and we might feel at the end of the book that God's people have finally arrived in the place of complete blessing and promised rest, led by the hero Joshua. Yet the book of Joshua does not end the story.

There are ominous shadows in the ending of this book. Joshua takes a large stone and tells the people he's setting it up "as a witness against you . . . lest you deal falsely with your God" (Josh. 24:27). In fact, at the end of Deuteronomy the Lord tells Moses that in their new land the people will "forsake me and break my covenant that I have made with them" (Deut. 31:16)—and Moses even tells the people about it in a song (Deut. 32). And, in fact, Judges informs us that the very next generation after the one that entered the land "did not know the LORD or the work that he had done for Israel" (Judg. 2:10). That the book of Joshua ends with his death emphasizes the fact that he—mighty leader and warrior that he was—could not lastingly accomplish the deliverance of blessing to the people.

Joshua, then, like the other parts of the Old Testament narrative, forces us to look ahead to find the perfect fulfillment to which it points. The *exodus* from slavery could finally be accomplished only by the blood of Jesus Christ the Lamb of God, who was sacrificed for our sins on the cross. The *law* could be completely fulfilled and obeyed only by the perfect Son of God, who himself was that perfect sacrifice. The *land* of rest, as a picture of the blessing of salvation enjoyed by God's people, could be delivered only by the final Joshua. That name *Joshua* means "The Lord saves" and in its Greek form is translated "Jesus."

The New Testament book of Hebrews helps us see the way Joshua even in his imperfection points ahead to the one who brought true, spiritual rest to God's people. The writer to the Hebrews speaks of the Sabbath rest that remains for the people of God, references David's call to hear God's voice "today," and comments, "For if Joshua had given them rest, God would not have spoken of another day later on" (Heb. 4:6–10). Yes, Joshua is about God's promises fulfilled—but it is not about the final fulfillment of them, which comes only in the final Joshua, who fought the greatest battle on our behalf so that we can enter into the eternal blessings of salvation. The book of Joshua ultimately leads us to seek God's promises not for rich land and battle victories, but rather for that rest of soul and ultimate rest of heaven promised to the followers of Jesus.

Ruth and Esther

Ruth and Esther are both easy to take utterly personally, as narratives that focus closely in on individuals and intimate relationships. The immediate and rather moralistic sort of application is that we should boldly trust God like these women did. That is true, although these women may not be examples for us in every way. That may not be the point.

In discussion of Ruth as narrative, we noticed that Ruth's story is encased in the larger story of Naomi. The whole narrative, actually, is encased in the even larger story of the generations of God's people leading up to that promised seed we have been talking about. Ruth follows the book of Judges, which begins with that ungodly generation after Joshua and ends with a final repetition of the desolate refrain, "Everyone did what was right in his own eyes" (Judg. 21:25). And then comes Ruth, which opens with Elimelech and his family, who are Ephrathites from Bethlehem in Judah. This is the city often associated with David, and this is the family line of Judah, David's line. It is not surprising, then, that the narrative concludes with an actual genealogy of David, placing Boaz and Ruth as his direct ancestors—thereby clarifying the line of Christ to which both ends of this story reach. This line, which represents God's promises being fulfilled, offers a thread of hope in an exceptionally dark part of the larger narrative. Even in the time of the judges, God was working out his promise that through Abraham's seed all nations of the world would be blessed.

This book offers a special perspective on the part of that promise regarding all nations. Ruth was not a Jew but a Moabitess who converted to Judaism. Moab in fact was a despised and idolatrous enemy of Israel. But God drew Ruth in from that ungodly nation, right into the center of the story. This drawing in from other nations shines out from this story—not just from Ruth, but from Boaz, whose mother, Rahab, was saved out of Jericho and also grafted into David's line, the line of Christ. The outermost edges of this story shimmer with the light of the gospel for all the nations, that gospel of Jesus Christ that Paul was called to preach but that long before Paul's time was showing the reach of God's grace into all the peoples of the world. The fact that Boaz is a kinsman-redeemer who spreads his wings in protection over Ruth does indeed reverberate with the larger truth of a Redeemer who spreads his wings over his called-out people, ultimately through the Promised One who descended from the characters in this story.

I recall a teaching session that focused on the person of Boaz and on his unselfish redemption of Ruth in chapter 4. We the listeners were asked to contrast Boaz with that unnamed closer kinsman-redeemer who had the first opportunity to redeem Ruth but didn't, fearing (ironically) that his own inheritance might be endangered. This was a helpful and enlightening contrast of characters. The application concerned the fact that we should think and be like Boaz instead of that other man, giving ourselves unselfishly to those around us in need, rather than protecting our own goods. We should be like Christ.

Helpful as that application was, mustn't we wonder if the whole story of Ruth and Naomi might cause us as careful readers to identify not as much with Boaz as with the women? Perhaps we should wonder not so much what was in Boaz's mind at this point (the narrative never goes there), but rather what was in Ruth's and Naomi's. Theirs is the experience of moving from empty to full, the movement that shapes the whole story. Theirs is the reaching out to ask for and to receive redemption, which here finally comes. In the actual redemption scene in chapter 4, Ruth and Naomi are silent. But this does not mean we should forget them and begin to identify suddenly with the men in the story who take center stage. The point is that this redemption is accomplished for these needy women by the one who is willing and able to do it: these women (and all of us) are the recipients of such covenant kindness.

Perhaps the application should ultimately involve a kind of wonder at such a Redeemer, who would draw under his wings needy people from all nations. Such an application might challenge us not only to grasp the nature of our salvation in Christ but also to be more impelled to share it with those whom God is today graciously drawing to himself from all the nations. These sorts of conclusions may not seem as personal as the more moralistic lessons, but in fact they are intensely personal, as we take in and learn to live out the implications of God's gospel promises.

The book of Esther works similarly, seemingly an isolated little narrative but actually a story full of glimmers of God's ongoing covenant promises to his people. The subplot of Haman, the bad guy, connects to the generation-long struggle between the Jews and the Amalekites, whose line God had promised (way back in Moses' and Joshua's day) to wipe off the face of the earth (Ex. 17:14–16). It was King Saul, we recall, who sinned in sparing the Amalekite King Agag, along with some of the cattle, after a victory in battle (see 1 Sam. 15). Centuries later, here in Susa pop up Mordecai, a direct descendant of King Saul (Esth. 2:5), and "Haman the Agagite" (Esth. 3:1), a leftover Amalekite trying to wipe out all the Jews in the Persian Empire. Not until the book of Esther is God's decree concerning this generational line fulfilled, as Haman is destroyed and his ten sons hanged—not in simple revenge but in fulfillment of God's word.

This story is much bigger than itself. The question of how God's people survived their years of exile and how the line of promise was not wiped out is answered concretely in Esther (and in Ezra and Nehemiah, the other exile narratives). God in his providence watched over his people, even through these years when they were scattered and seemingly impotent, and even when he seemed absent . . . one notices, of course, that God's name is not mentioned in the book of Esther. However, in the context of the larger story, we can affirm that God is clearly at work, sovereignly accomplishing all his promises. Not only are the Jews saved in Esther, but we read that "many from the peoples of the country declared themselves Jews, for fear of the Jews had fallen on them" (Esth. 8:17). The promise of blessing to the nations through Abraham's descendants continues to bear fruit, as that promise moves inexorably toward its ultimate fulfillment in Christ.

Should we want to be like Esther? Or Ruth? Or Boaz? In some ways, yes. The focus of attention in these stories, however, is on the remarkable weaving together of the narrative both within the book and in the larger context. In fact, we should come away mostly amazed at the way God is weaving the whole big story together according to his covenant promises, detail after detail and generation after generation. We should be both humbled and encouraged that God would take such care with our stories. We should wonder at the way he includes and uses us in his huge, gracious plan of salvation that is ultimately all about his Son. I can't imagine a greater encouragement for us here, now, to trust and faithfully follow a sovereign God who is weaving together all of history for his redemptive purposes.

"Many people I encounter have very little knowledge of history. They live in the moment. Life is all about here and now, you and me, our interests. This means they have a difficult time understanding the Bible as a historical document—the inspired record of God's dealing with mankind from one end of human history to the other. They don't see themselves as necessarily connected with folks who have gone before them and folks who will come after them."

—Carol Ruvolo, author and Bible study leader, Heritage Christian Fellowship, Albuquerque, New Mexico

---

Psalms and Proverbs

The promise of Jesus the Savior shines out of the heart of the psalms, a good number of which directly point to the coming Messiah. We have seen Psalm 16 and Psalm 22 as good examples. Psalm 77 we have described as not directly messianic—and this is true for many of the psalms. But all the psalms reach out to Christ in one way or another.

The psalms are the prayers and praises of God's people mostly from the period when they were a nation under a king. The kingdom offers another picture of salvation history, as we glimpse (especially in the flourishing days of Solomon) the beauty of God's people gathered together in the land of his promise under the rule of his anointed king. We know, however, that the kings were imperfect, and we know about the eventual split and decline and fall of the kingdoms. After the exile, there was no longer any king. The history of the kingdom should make us both celebrate the wonder of a glorious king and also yearn for a perfect king. This is the kind of celebration and yearning that fills the psalms, with all of it ultimately reaching out to Christ the perfect King, who came to save and to rule forever.

Starting with Psalm 1, a single perfect man looms. We noted the singular "man" who stands against the plural wicked ones. Throughout the poetic literature we hear a call to follow the righteous way as opposed to the wicked way, and yet we consistently face head-on our own inability to do so. The penitential psalms (of confession) acknowledge our unrighteousness before a holy God. We keep encountering this righteous man who offers the standard—a standard we know we cannot reach. Who has not at some point quaked at statements like these:

> Blessed is the man who fears the LORD,
> who greatly delights in his commandments!
> . . . .
> Light dawns in the darkness for the upright;
> he is gracious, merciful, and righteous.
> . . . .
> For the righteous will never be moved;
> he will be remembered forever. (Ps. 112:1, 4, 6)

Having heard of that man, some readers might be slow to step up and respond to calls like the one that begins Psalm 33: "Shout for joy in the LORD, O you righteous!" Here, perhaps, is one instance where the order of the psalms has significance. Psalm 32 presents one of the most beautiful prayers of offering confession and finding forgiveness. Only after that process, in the psalm's final verse, are the "upright in heart" called to shout for joy—which connects directly to the opening call of Psalm 33.

The psalms never tell us just how sin is forgiven by a holy God; we know only that when we truly confess he forgives sin, covers it, doesn't count it against us (Ps. 32:1–2). Sacrifices for sin are mentioned. But there's sort of a logical knot in the psalms concerning exactly how the sin of a repentant person is wiped clean before a holy God. This is where the figure of the man looms most large. Different aspects of him emerge. The man is righteous unlike any other man we know. The man suffers greater depths of suffering than we can imagine (as in Psalm 22). The man is a deliverer-king greater than any we have ever known (see Psalm 72).

The man is Jesus. Only through the life and death of such a perfect sacrifice can the wrath of a holy God be satisfied. Only through his righteousness can we be made righteous. The pieces are all there in the psalms, but they have not all come together clearly and by the name of Jesus. The psalms reach out to him, both directly and indirectly, with longing for the righteous Savior-King who would finally come and accomplish our salvation.

The Wisdom Literature reaches out similarly. Proverbs offers a good example as it paints the picture of wisdom lived out in the kingdom of God's people. The question arises: If Jesus is not directly mentioned in Proverbs, how does this book point to him? Is this not a book of general wisdom, which would be read quite similarly by people who don't believe in Christ and people who do? The answer is partly yes, in that Proverbs shows the world to be set up according to certain moral principles that apply to everybody who lives in this world. But the answer is mostly no, in that the truth of the gospel of Jesus Christ inevitably shines through this book as well.

Proverbs makes immediately clear its context of God's people living in his kingdom: the book begins, "The proverbs of Solomon, son of David, king of Israel." This kingdom context is the only context where this wisdom ultimately makes sense. Only under the rule of God's anointed king can the laws that God originally set up be perfectly lived out. The basic concept of wisdom unfolds throughout Scripture and cannot be separated from the New Testament's clear pointing to the "anointed one," which means "the Christ"—"Christ Jesus, who became to us wisdom from God" (1 Cor. 1:30). According to all of Scripture, wisdom is ultimately found in a person and in a relationship, not in a concept or a principle. It makes sense, then, that Proverbs starts out with the fear of the LORD as the beginning of the whole process (Prov. 1:7). Clues to the personal nature of wisdom abound in the book, even through its imagery that pictures wisdom as a living being who works and speaks and calls us to herself.

Perhaps the most climactic clues come in Proverbs 8, where the personification of wisdom speaks in some of the most glorious poetry ever composed. As wisdom tells of being there with God in creation, "beside him, like a master workman" (Prov. 8:30), we peer into this mysterious poetry and again see in the background a looming figure, one to whom this voice is pointing, the Son of God, who is the only source of wisdom from before the foundations of the earth. Derek Kidner points to the "wider setting" indicated specifically by the poetry of Proverbs 8 (I include all his Scripture references to show the connections he draws throughout the New Testament):

The New Testament shows by its allusions to this passage (Col. 1:15–17; 2:3; Rev. 3:14) that the personifying of wisdom, far from overshooting the literal truth, was a preparation for its full statement, since the agent of creation was no mere activity of God, but the Son, His eternal Word, Wisdom and Power (see also Jn. 1:1–14; 1 Cor. 1:24, 30; Heb. 1:1–4).[1]

This big perspective on Proverbs makes all the difference in applying it. We can grit our teeth and try as hard as we can to live out the principles Proverbs teaches. This is what many nonbelievers have done; it can help, but it will finally frustrate. As believers, we can hear and heed Proverbs' call to focus on our relationship to the personal source of all wisdom, and so through his saving power learn to live out wisdom as we live in him and under his kingly rule.

The Prophets, Isaiah in Particular

We have looked at implications of Scripture's storyline in narrative and poetic Old Testament passages. What about the Prophets? In one sense, the Prophets are known for their pointing toward Christ with specific words from God that Jesus comes and fulfills. For example, many know Isaiah's prophecy concerning Immanuel (Isa. 7:14), which Matthew 1:20–23 tells us is directly fulfilled in Christ. Daniel's vision of the glorious king who appears as "one like a son of man" (Dan. 7:13) points clearly to Jesus, who used that title *Son of Man* often to refer to himself.

The last Old Testament prophet, Malachi, ends his prophecy looking forward to the "sun of righteousness" who "shall rise with healing in its wings" and also to Elijah the prophet who will come before (Mal. 4). John the Baptist's father, Zechariah, evidently knew this passage and others that emerge clearly in the beautiful words that pour from him at the birth of his son, who is called to prepare the way before Jesus (Luke 1:68–79). The Old Testament ends with the Prophets leaning forward to see the great plan of salvation accomplished in the one who looms larger and larger on the horizon.

As we said, the first role of the prophets was to speak God's word to God's people in that place and time. They were not all about prophesying the future. And yet their words regularly reach out to Christ. We might say "reach out" as well as "reach ahead," for the reality of Christ and the presence of Christ were not only not future but also present, even for them. They did not yet know Christ incarnate, but the second person of the Trinity was present and active in their lives, as he has always been present and active from eternity past. Christ is not a new character who enters the story in the New Testament. Peter clearly teaches the early church about the active presence and work of Christ among his people even before he appeared in the flesh:

> Concerning this salvation, the prophets who prophesied about the grace that was to be yours searched and inquired carefully, inquiring what person or time the Spirit of Christ in them was indicating when he predicted the suffering of Christ and the subsequent glories. (1 Peter 1:10–11)

Isaiah offers some of the most vivid Old Testament glimpses of the Messiah to come. A thorough study would require many books, and indeed many books have been written—one of the best by Alec Motyer, who masterfully combines a thorough examination of the text with an eye to the whole Scriptures. Motyer is one of a number of commentators who see three messianic portraits dominating three main sections of Isaiah: the King (Isa. 1–37), the Servant (Isa. 38–55), and the Conqueror (Isa. 56–66).[2] Even this brief outline of Isaiah alerts us to the fact that careful study of the book itself leads to the best kind of connection with Christological meaning. We too often tend to extract Isaiah's famous forward-looking passages from their contexts, pulling them out for special seasons like Christmas and Easter.

The four "Servant Songs" in the middle of the book include many of these more well-known passages that should be enjoyed all together and in their context, not just in extracted fragments. In these songs (so called because they stand out in their beauty and thematic unity) the person and work of Jesus truly emerge. It was the fourth song, from Isaiah 53, that the Ethiopian eunuch was trying vainly to understand, until Philip came and helped him: "Then Philip opened his mouth, and beginning with this Scripture he told him the good news about Jesus" (Acts 8:35).

It is beautiful to watch the process of Jesus emerging from these songs as they build on and harmonize with each other, with a whole orchestra surrounding them. There are actually two singers who together step forth to sing these songs. They are like two soloists in a concerto, and the orchestra's part, the music in which their songs are embedded, is a section of Isaiah that focuses on the suffering of God's people in exile as punishment for their sin. The whole concerto is embedded in the larger context of a book all about God's plan of salvation. In these songs the accomplishment of that promised salvation is revealed to God's suffering people. The nation of God's people, whom God also calls his "servant" and even his "son" at various points, needs to see the suffering of the one perfect servant on their behalf: this is how their promised salvation will be accomplished.

- In the *first song* (Isa. 42:1–9), the Lord speaks ("Behold my servant . . ."). He points to one who is there with him, one we can just glimpse there in the shadows, a servant chosen by God to bring about God's justice in surprising, lowly ways.

- In the *second song* (Isa. 49:1–6), the servant himself steps out of the shadows and speaks ("Listen to me . . ."), and the Word with a "mouth like a sharp sword" tells of his suffering and yet the encouragement of his Father.
- In the *third song* (Isa. 50:4–9), the servant reveals the full suffering of his passion, with that beautiful refrain shining out of the midst of the pain: "But the Lord GOD helps me."
- In the *final song* (Isa. 52:13–53:12), the servant steps back into the shadows, to be fully revealed at the proper time. God resumes the speaking role, telling the mysteries of his sovereign plan of redemption, which includes not only the suffering and death of this servant but also his resurrection and the life of many offspring.

Each of these songs is followed in the text by a response of praise, which feels like the whole orchestra coming in after the soloists' parts. These responses become our responses as we gradually take in this revelation of Father and Son singing together of the mysteries of salvation in a kind of heavenly duet. Such passages stretch our minds, our imaginations, and our prayers.

The whole story is all about Jesus. The more we study the story's parts, the more we see Jesus Christ shining from every nook and cranny. The more we see him at the heart of the story, the more we understand how the story is hurtling forward toward the end, when every eye shall see him, every knee bow, "and every tongue confess that Jesus Christ is Lord, to the glory of God the Father" (Phil. 2:10–11; Rev. 1:7).

9

So . . .

What Is Bible Study?

Taking in the Scriptures with:

1. The five truths as starting points
2. Ongoing leadership training
3. Flexibility of implementation

HAVING MADE OUR WAY THROUGH all these truths and implications of truths concerning the Bible, we arrive at the somewhat audacious question: What is Bible study? What is that cluster of elements that defines it? Who's to say? Can't Bible study mean a lot of different things? Christian fellowship can mean a lot of different things. Bible study, however, is a more distinct activity and so can be defined more distinctly. If what we have said about the Bible is true, and if the implications we have drawn are valid, then these truths and implications must dramatically affect our understanding of Bible study.

Perhaps part of our problem is that we have simply not been careful with our terms. A group that meets primarily for sharing and prayer is an invaluable fellowship opportunity but probably shouldn't be called a Bible study. Our carelessness with terms has evolved at least partly because Bible study groups have sometimes evolved into fellowship groups . . . it's just easier! Nobody has to prepare in depth, and everybody can share and be affirmed. It is important here to be clear and to affirm wholeheartedly that groups centered on sharing and prayer are absolutely wonderful. But surely they shouldn't replace Bible study. Often they can profitably join up with Bible study, especially if there are leaders who are trained and watching for the right balance. Our prayers should indeed grow out of our study of the Word.

If Bible study is a distinct activity, how, after all this discussion of the Bible, should we finally define it? Before suggesting a definition, some acknowledgments are in order—the first and greatest being the fact that I'm keenly aware of how many people there are with wisdom to offer and corrections to make in regard to this discussion. That's why I have incorporated comments of other people involved in Bible study. Let me acknowledge as well that the definition I will offer makes a stab at a kind of ideal—Bible study as it should be. We will not always attain such an ideal. But we can work toward such an ideal. The first step is talking about it and helping each other get it somewhat clear. We all know that if we aim nowhere, we will get there. It is important for those of us involved in Bible study to consider and discuss these things, especially given the increasing fuzziness about the subject in many circles.

One final acknowledgment, or perhaps qualification: I am speaking specifically of Bible study led by those who believe in the biblical gospel of Jesus Christ. Of course, unbelievers in many contexts take up the Scriptures and investigate them in a variety of ways for a variety of purposes, including scholarly study, simple curiosity, or anti-Christian research. Some of them come to Christ in the process, for the Word is powerful and will accomplish whatever God intends in whatever way he directs. And we hope there will be unbelievers in Bible studies led by believers—unbelievers we hope will come to believe. With this definition I speak to the audience defined from the beginning: the body of Christ, those primarily responsible for Bible study.

What is Bible study? In the context of the acknowledgments made, let me suggest a definition with three elements. *Bible study is an activity in which we take in the Scriptures with the truths we have discussed as starting points, with leaders trained in these truths, and with flexibility of implementation of these truths.*

The Five Truths as Starting Points

I stated back at the beginning of chapter 1 that perhaps the most basic element in the cluster of characteristics essential for Bible study is a clear understanding and communication of what Scripture is. The ensuing chapters have explored five truths: that the Bible is God speaking; that the Bible is powerful; that the Bible is understandable; that the Bible is a literary work; and that the Bible is one story. From these truths have emerged clear implications for our study of such a book.

131

The distinctive of this approach is that it begins with the Bible itself and what it asks of us, rather than with what we need and would like to "get out of" Bible study. Many Bible study groups these days start with some sort of poll, seeking to know what the people in the group desire from the study, and then the study is designed or chosen according to that poll. It is indeed good to know a group and its needs and desires. But it is also important to recall that what every human being needs most fundamentally is to hear God's voice—to take in the food of his Word, which is a more basic need even than daily bread.

The most foundational premise, however, is not the nature of our need. The most foundational premise is the nature of God and of his Word. Even a glimpse of who God is and what it means that he speaks to us leads to the logical response of respect for and submission to his words. This is in the end a matter of recognizing the authority of the God of the universe, whose word matters and whose word rules. Many have noted the fact that "understanding" a biblical text means "standing under" it—that is, submitting ("putting under") ourselves to it. The process of working hard to understand the meaning God intended—through the themes and shape and vocabulary and grammar and imagery and all the rest of it—is part of our submission to a Word that comes to us from the one in charge.

Sometimes what we find hard about studying Scripture has to do with more than the difficulty of finding a text's meaning. At least as often, I suspect, what we find hard is that Scripture tells us things that make us uncomfortable. Most of us would rather study things that make us comfortable than submit ourselves to a book with many parts that don't.

We imagined at the start a picture of a bridge across which a speaker sends words to be received on the other side. Perhaps we should adjust that picture and make it a bridge reaching down from heaven. To receive the words God sends us with the meaning he intends requires that we bend down low at the foot of the bridge and look up to receive the words. I do not spend time on these truths and their implications in order to set up a complicated system that we must follow in order to be well educated in the Scriptures. Rather, I am suggesting that we all need to spend time learning and relishing and teaching these truths in order to establish together a right starting point for taking in the words of life that God in his mercy speaks to us. They are in the end words of life and delight—even the ones that make us uncomfortable as we take them in. If they are living and active and true and powerful, as God says, then we can trust them to accomplish God's good and gracious purposes in our lives as we humbly receive them.

Many books on Bible study include large and helpful sections on group dynamics. Some training sessions for Bible study leaders focus on group dynamics more than on the subjects discussed in this book. The argument would be that if we can draw people in and make them feel comfortable and affirmed, then we have accomplished the most important thing; they'll probably stay, they'll be loved and prayed for, and they will be open to taking in whatever is taught. Group dynamics are important. I believe we should train leaders in this area and pray earnestly about these matters. But I don't believe we should make these matters our starting point or our main focus in training Bible study leaders.

Training for Bible study best starts with the Bible itself—what's true about it and what we know about its words. From these truths flow what we are called to do in Bible study, how we should do it, and the power to accomplish it as the Spirit works. As the Spirit applies Scripture's words to people's hearts in the course of studying it, they are being loved and their needs met in the deepest way—a way that should be reinforced and acted out by the love of fellow group members. The kind of humility we have talked about ("standing under" the Word, in light of these truths about the Word) revolutionizes group dynamics as we together learn to listen humbly to God and to each other. Setting these truths about the Word as our starting point for Bible study makes a world of difference.

Ongoing Leadership Training

The concept of leadership training has been explicitly and implicitly woven into everything stated so far. Affirming these truths about Scripture as a starting point implies that the leaders of any kind of Bible study group should be taught these truths by other leaders who have learned them. These truths and their implications for Bible study have been graciously taught and modeled before me in a whole variety of ways, and I am grateful.

"What makes any context for Bible study a successful one is, first of all, leadership. The old saying holds true: As the leader goes, so goes the group."

—Mary Beth McGreevy, Visiting Instructor, Covenant Theological Seminary, St. Louis, Missouri

We all bring our special backgrounds and experiences to enrich this training, but we all need some basic training in Bible study. Given what we have said about the need to study hard and carefully, with detailed attention to main idea, words, shape, genre, narrative unity, etc., it is clear that these necessary parts of Bible study will not usually just happen if a well-intentioned group simply gets together to talk over a passage without the presence of a trained leader. We saw those leaders in Nehemiah moving among the people and explaining the sense of what was being read, so that they could understand. That is a good model. We have asserted that Scripture is understandable. But we have also asserted the need for us to give ourselves wholeheartedly to the process and labor of understanding.

We have said no from the start to the question of whether these trained leaders should be only formally educated pastors and biblical scholars. These leaders have a huge responsibility, and we should respect and pray for them, particularly the pastoral leaders in our local congregations who carry the huge responsibility of preaching the Word in season and out of season. Paul's words are strong: "We ask you, brothers, to respect those who labor among you and are over you in the Lord and admonish you, and to esteem them very highly in love because of their work" (1 Thess. 5:12–13). Clearly, the need to train many leaders within the church does not imply any lessening of the authority or lessening of respect for the authority of pastors and elders.

In fact, the need for training implies an opportunity for pastors and all other leaders to share their good recipes rather than exhausting themselves by doing all the cooking. The underlying motive is not about who gets to have the recipes; the motive is all about the fact that there are many to feed, and many more, by God's grace, coming in to be fed. We should all be ready to feed others with what we have been fed. I do not mean that we should all be pastors who preach; that is a distinct calling in itself. But certainly we should all be increasingly equipped to speak and share the Word. Training up its members gives an opportunity for the church to grow in the Word, to follow the directive of the Great Commission, and to participate fruitfully together in the multiplication of disciples.

This discussion points to the context of the church—both the church universal and the local church. All members of the church universal have been given this book of Scripture to believe and learn and love and study and obey and share. And each member of the church universal is called, according to the teaching of the Word, to live in fellowship with a local body of Christians, a local church. Bible study can, of course, happen apart from the local church. Some independent Bible study groups have come to exist perhaps partly because the local church was not hospitable to the work and training of Bible study. Some have established strong leadership structures of their own in order to protect their biblical and theological foundations. Many have been powerfully used by God to spread his Word.

It seems to me, however, that the most logical and powerful place for Bible study to grow and prosper is within the local church. This context provides crucial biblical oversight from church leadership, especially in the process of training. It also offers an opportunity for coherent ministry among families of Bible study participants, as well as a church home ready to welcome those who come to faith through Bible study and need to be "plugged in" to the body.

Pastors have been mentioned specifically in connection with the local church, because training seems to happen best when it happens through a church's pastoral leadership. If training happens apart from existing leadership, that training can easily be perceived as threatening, subversive, and harmful, even if it is not meant that way. Or it can simply be biblically unsound, depending on its origin.

I have observed many women's Bible study groups, for example, that are basically "doing their own thing," quite separate from the oversight of the leadership of the church. Sometimes those groups are doing fine. And sometimes they're not. Sometimes they're doing better than the rest of the church, and the church could benefit from their vision. But sometimes they need clarification of vision themselves. It is a blessing for church members and church groups to receive training that grows from the vision and even the active participation of pastors. The result is that the church members know, love, and respect their pastors more; that they are more biblically and consistently trained; and that more people are then able to be effectively led in all kinds of Bible study, whether it be one-on-one discipleship, Sunday school classes, or Bible study groups.

A pastor or even most pastoral staffs cannot lead twenty different weekly Bible studies, but they can train twenty leaders to lead those groups—and those twenty leaders can pass it on. The point in relation to the women's Bible study example would not be to have the pastor regularly teach the women's Bible study. He more than likely does not have time. The point would be rather for the leadership of the church to invest in ongoing training that will produce biblically grounded women who can teach and lead with excellence and help others learn to do the same.

One church I visited had sent their women's ministry director off to seminary, paid for her degree, and received her back ready to serve. It doesn't always have to happen that way, but making that investment surely showed the church's commitment to raising up strong, biblical leadership among the congregation. Some churches offer leadership-track classes for men and women interested in various positions of leadership—classes such as Biblical Theology, Systematic Theology, Bible Overview, How to Read and Study the Bible, Romans, etc.

Colin Marshall and Tony Payne have been thinking about and implementing such ideas for a number of years. Their book, *The Trellis and the Vine: The Ministry Mind-Shift That Changes Everything*, argues clearly and biblically for the need to train up believers in the Word. Basically, they picture many contemporary pastors spending more energy on an elaborate but inanimate trellis (i.e., church programs and events) than on the living vine that should be growing on the trellis (i.e., training disciples to grow in the Word and multiply that growth). Marshall and Payne describe their vision this way: "What we are really talking about is a Bible-reading movement—in families, in churches, in neighborhoods, in workplaces, everywhere. Imagine if all Christians, as a normal part of their discipleship, were caught up in a web of regular Bible reading."[1] They claim that such a vision will come to pass in large part through training:

> Training is the engine of gospel growth. Under God, the way to get more gospel growth happening is to train more and more mature, godly Christians to be vine-workers—that is, to see more people equipped, resourced and encouraged to speak the word prayerfully to other people, whether in outreach, follow-up or Christian growth.[2]

These two writers and their mentors have greatly influenced some of those who have been my pastors—and I can see their influence extended to me as well. The vine grows!

The lovely aspect of such ongoing training is that its fruit spreads near and far. I have focused on the context of more formal Bible study groups, but of course Bible study happens in all kinds of contexts, from the kitchen table at home to one-on-one meetings to all kinds of classes and groups. The training received by individuals is carried not only into the activity of Bible study itself but into many kinds of interactions—with family, with friends and neighbors, in classrooms, at work, and on and on.

"A commitment to training teachers keeps the reality of preparing the next generation in the forefronts of the minds of our leadership team. There is an argument to be made for the depth of insight that experienced, mature, teachers-that-make-videos could bring to women of our church, but I remain convinced that by training teachers within our own body we are sowing the seeds of spiritual maturity that will reap a harvest for generations to come."

—Teren Sechrist, Bible study teacher, Berean Baptist Church, Livonia, Michigan

---

Flexibility of Implementation

The third and final element of our definition of Bible study acknowledges that there is not one set way to make all this happen. We can affirm everything we have said so far and also affirm that the implementation of everything said so far may take different forms. The truths and implications discussed must work together, sometimes in different orders. A leader who has studied these truths will come to a particular text and be able to see and deal with that text in light of them, rather than applying a fixed formula of questions and methods. We should start with the text itself as much as possible, following its lead.

Beginning with that first crucial step of observation opens the way for such flexibility: If observation leads to noticing a repeated refrain in a passage, then that refrain, and that passage's configuration around that refrain, may be important to notice early on in grappling with the main idea. If observation leads to noticing a central character and the way in which he or she is presented, then the character question may be a fruitful early route into the text. If there is powerful imagery that stands out, that may call for early or consistent attention. Noticing imagery may lead to noticing genre, which may help open up a text.

"Sitting next to the left-brained learner is your typical right-brained learner, who rushed in just a wee bit late, forgot his or her Bible, has a funny story to share before the group begins, and can't wait for the first break so that he or she can meet and greet the other members. He or she loves a good story that helps get a point across, rarely looks at an outline, and likes lots of audiovisuals, group discussions, and opportunities for creative expression."

—Jane S. Craig, Ph.D., educator, member of Rincon Mountain Presbyterian Church, Tucson, Arizona

---

Different individuals and groups will also have different levels of experience in study, as well as different tolerance for hard work. For a group not used to the hard work of study, it might be beneficial for a leader to help them actively and to choose materials that help them actively, especially at the start, so that their confidence will grow and they will be more open to learning how to dig in themselves. This is why we need people as leaders, rather than just recorded or written materials. There is no substitute for fellow imperfect human beings showing us what they've learned and working flexibly with various kinds of learners. There's no substitute for a good (live!) leader who can point the way into a text and deal on the spot with the questions of a unique group. There's no substitute for the person-to-person discipleship that tends to reproduce itself when one person learns from another, prays for another, and grows with another in the Word.

This flexible process can happen in a variety of ways. In an ideal world, everybody involved in the same Bible study would spend daily concentrated time working on a passage. They would all then come together regularly to share the fruit of their study, led by a trained person who has studied the passage in depth and is ready to lead others in processing it and pulling together what they have learned. Everyone knows how challenging it is these days to require such faithfulness and depth of study; however, establishing the ideal is important. There will always be those who catch on to it and who strive for it, not necessarily because of a superior work ethic or a studious bent (although God can use such things) but because God's Word will powerfully work in his people and lead them to love it and to desire it more and more, as they through it love him and desire him more and more.

We should remind ourselves that the truths we've discussed are truly true! We can depend on them—particularly on the power of this Word that God speaks to us. I've seen women with unbelievably busy lives—perhaps with many small children or consuming work—systematically order their lives to include the essential of Bible study in one form or another. If we have a throbbing toothache, we simply order our lives around that essential trip to the dentist. It's a matter of what's essential.

"In one form or another" truly means just that! Most often, people do need accountability, as well as the wisdom of another, and so whatever form evolves will and perhaps should involve communication and interaction with another person or two or more. During one of my high school years, a friend named Elsbeth (with whom I had served on staff at a summer Bible conference) and I mailed weekly to each other pages of notes we were making on the book of Romans, a passage at a time. There was actually something satisfying about the commitment to put that letter in the mailbox each week—and to find hers. We learned a lot from each other that year.

"Bible study allows a gradual process to take place in people's lives, and an ongoing context in which lives can change. Of course, a context in which there is community and account- ability, and in which people feel loved and cared for, is major in allowing the good seed to be planted, take root, flourish, and then multiply."

—anonymous pastor, serving in East Asia

The ideal form, however, does involve a trained leader who can help others study effectively. If the truths and implications we have discussed are valid, then surely it follows that there are better ways to study and less helpful ways to study, even with flexibility of implementation. Studying without attention to context is definitely less helpful. So is a lack of understanding of poetic form and imagery or a failure to draw the conclusions and applications that truly grow out of the text. A well-trained leader can encourage those studying to look for . . . shall we say the "right" things? This book has surely not adequately covered all the "right" things, and these truths and principles will surely lead people to discover and articulate what they learn in Scripture in a whole variety of ways. Yet it does seem possible to say, on the ground of Scripture itself, that we are called to approach it in certain ways. By a "right" approach to Scripture we must finally mean not simply "factually correct" or "correct according to someone's good system," but rather "pleasing and obedient to the God who spoke these words."

How does a well-trained leader encourage those studying to look for the right things, while remaining flexible? He or she can do that by effectively leading a discussion, summing up a discussion, giving a formal teaching, or combining these activities. As a teacher, I have always valued teaching by a trained person who has studied and who willingly shares the fruit of that training and study with a group who has also been studying and is primed to listen and learn. But I am learning that formal teaching does not always work. Large groups do not always work. Effective discussion-leading is sometimes the most viable route.

Some would claim that formal teaching no longer works as effectively as it used to because people these days are not as willing to study and not as open to receive teaching. There may be some truth to that claim; we have discussed Bible study in relation to contemporary views of authority. According to my observation, teaching is more readily accepted and

143

celebrated in contexts where there is clear leadership vision and good training—often accompanied by encouragement of teaching.

Another factor may be at work—that of different generations working together. Some would claim that many of the changes and tensions we're talking about simply result from a younger generation's different ways of going about things. We'll get to this in the next chapter. Having laid forth this definition of Bible study—an activity in which we take in the Scriptures with the truths we have discussed as starting points, with leaders trained in these truths, and with flexibility of implementation of these truths—we are now ready for a final look at the future challenge and promise of Bible study.

10

Looking Ahead . . .

The Challenge

The Challenge:

1. Generational opportunities
2. Getting outside ourselves
3. Nothing new

LOOKING INTO THE FUTURE OF BIBLE STUDY, we should see great challenge and great promise. The promise meets and over-whelms the challenge. But first, let's discuss the challenge.

Generational Opportunities

We referred in the last chapter to generational tensions in relation to Bible study. It's a commonly discussed subject, as people almost compulsively analyze the move from baby

145

boomers to Generation Xers to Millennials to whoever's coming next. The church is the beautiful mix of all these generations, which we should mainly celebrate rather than worry about. However, discernible general differences do exist, and we should be aware of them as part of the challenge that not only can be met but also can enrich Bible study.

The stereotypical illustration sets up, on the one hand, the older folks all dressed up for a carefully planned event with decorated tables and a special speaker, and on the other hand the younger folks, who are more casually dressed, cell phones in hand, wanting more than anything else to enjoy some interaction with peers. It is true that, in general, older people have more experience with listening to teachers and speakers, and younger people have lived through a transition into a format of more interaction and less instruction. Sermons in general have shortened in length; many people do not want to sit and listen for longer than perhaps twenty minutes. College classes these days on the whole involve much less of a straight lecture format and much more interactive and collaborative learning than several decades ago.

The reasons for these shifts are certainly complex, but of course the first cause mentioned usually relates to technology. The bare fact that people have developed the ability to communicate with as many people as they wish, whenever and wherever, has revolutionized the nature of our interactions. The presence of a universe of information available at the touch of a button is empowering and consuming. Amid all this live interaction our minds now seem to move more readily in the form of many quick spurts from one subject or person to another, rather than through long, steady trains of thought in one direction. We more and more tend to embrace rather than try to resolve the ambiguity of multiple perspectives. With the possibility of e-mailing, texting, tweeting, etc., we can easily and quickly insert all our immediate thoughts into the series of spurts that keep our minds hopping like a succession of quick features on a cable news show—always up against a break.

Here's the generality (which means that it's often true but certainly not always): the younger the people with whom we're interacting, the more comfortable with all this change they will tend to be; the older the people, the less comfortable they will tend to be. In my experience, it is true that many people of retirement age have learned to use technology, but many are uncomfortable with it. The "baby boomers" have learned to use technology and are much more comfortable with it, often amazed by it. The "Generation Xers" delight in technology and use it proficiently. With the "new millennials" (whom I meet in the college community of which I am a part), this kind of talk does not even compute: technology is not something objective to evaluate but rather the air they breathe. These are the trends.[1]

"A young Director of Women's Ministry gave me this illustration: older women in a Bible study quickly land on a theologically correct statement, while the younger generation likes to take off in an airplane, circle the question, take plenty of time, and eventually (not always) land on truth . . . it's all about process for them."

—Jane Patete, Women's Ministries Coordinator,
Presbyterian Church in America

I take the time to consider all this because we should realize and discuss the challenge these trends bring to the activity of

Bible study. No easy answers exist. Actually, instead of offering answers, I would suggest adjusting the questions we ask. The question I hear most frequently in relation to this generational dilemma is the question of how Bible studies should change in order to adjust to a different generation. All of us are and should be concerned not to lose the younger generation in the church. It's a huge issue. Many young people are leaving the church. And so we ask, in this context, "How can we adapt to younger generations in order to make them feel comfortable and at home?"

This is a great question, but it's perhaps not the first one we should ask. Or perhaps it's just part of what we should ask. What happens if we consider this generational challenge in light of what we have asserted about Bible study as an activity for taking in the Scriptures with the truths we have discussed as starting points, with leaders trained in these truths, and with flexibility of implementation of these truths? If these elements of Bible study are our starting point, then the generational question will be one of relating this starting point to a varied and changing audience. On the one hand, we have a question that has the audience and the methods as starting points, and on the other hand, we have a question that has as its starting point commitments about the Bible and about leading people to understand it more fully.

Perhaps in planning Bible study we need to ask which we trust more: our methods of reaching people or the truths about the Word and its power to speak into people's lives. These two factors are obviously both important; it's just a matter of which comes first. Flexibility of implementation *of these foundational truths and implications* has to exist. However, if we aim to build on these truths and their implications, the goal will be to adjust in light of them, rather than to adjust simply in

148

light of a new generation's needs. Considering this question with a different premise might lead us to some of the same ends, but perhaps not all.

If the younger generation is less oriented to following the lead of a teacher and more oriented to a discussion format, how should the church respond? Are there ways that we can meet people's need for more interaction, while still leading a group toward more and more in-depth study of the words of Scripture? How can we creatively provide ways for trained leaders to lead others in following these truths and implications for study? Do some of the implications we have discussed necessitate longer periods of concentrated work on one text than many people are used to? I believe there are ways to answer these questions, but ways not aimed primarily toward making people comfortable—rather, ways aimed primarily toward hearing God speak through his Word.

Of course, we are not talking about unloving methods vs. loving methods. Too often that dichotomy gets made, and unfortunately it has in some cases been proved true. Certainly all would agree that believers must never focus on communicating the content of the Word without at the same time focusing on living it out personally, with loving compassion and care. In chapter 1 we talked about the personal nature of the Word and of studying the Word; clearly, this activity is personal and relational at its core. The foundational assumption, according to the Word itself, is that no matter what our methods, our interactions should be full of the compassion and love of God.

Having clarified that assumption, we can go on to say that what the younger generation most desperately needs (and what all of us need) is to hear God speak. We need to believe the psalmist's words: "How can a young man keep his way pure? By guarding it according to your word" (Ps. 119:9). The power of God's Word in their lives, by the Spirit, in the context of a loving body, will call young people to stay in the church. Teaching them the Bible from an early age may be ultimately the most loving and compassionate thing we can do. That God speaks is both the premise and the goal of Bible study. It is the overwhelming truth that should shape our questions about how to study the Bible.

If God speaks and through his Word points centrally to his Son, then we should constantly remind ourselves that our central aim is to believe him, follow him, and together conform ourselves to his image. That aim, instead of dividing us into generational categories, brings us together as human beings desperately in need of God's saving and empowering Word. That aim brings us together and lets us ask what characteristics we all have that we need either to lay down as sinful or to offer as helpful. The characteristics of generations are not always morally neutral, so that we should simply say, "Look, this is the way it is. Let's adjust." Should we not evaluate all these characteristics in light of the Word?

Older people can hugely benefit from the openness and vulnerability of younger people, learning from them to lay down what is sometimes a selfish concern for privacy or structure or image and to open themselves more fully to serving others in every way. Sometimes openness to complexity and ambiguity in place of too-simple answers is called for. Many younger people have taught me much in these areas, and I have much to learn. It is also true that younger people often need to learn the unselfishness of being quiet and listening, the discipline of long, concentrated work in one direction, and the actual possibility of embracing truth instead of courting doubt.

Older people and younger people profit from being together in studying the Bible so that different tendencies

150

can be shared, celebrated, and examined. We can see and help each other better when we're not all seeing from the same context. In my experience what tends to happen is that the more we step across those generational divides, the more we find that the stereotypes and generalities do not apply. The problems we attribute to generational differences may sometimes have as much to do with our assumptions about generational differences. We all surely have known many young people with hearts of steadfast faith in God's truth and with an amazing thirst for deep, concentrated study, including study of the Bible. We all have known those older people who are always ready to talk about anything ad infinitum or who find it hard to settle down to long listening or study. We're all learning and growing!

There is no one true "baby boomer" or "Generation Xer"; there are only individual people, who are all different and who all need to take in God's Word as their life and light. We are all being sanctified as God's people, by God's grace. One would hope that if we truly believe in the process of sanctification, we would all look for and be able to find those older believers who have the wisdom of years with the Lord and who will share that wisdom with us. But we all have much to share. The generations will keep changing, as they always have. Human beings will be different and yet the same. Perhaps the key is to see human beings more and more in light of the Bible's whole big story we've been talking about, with Jesus Christ at the center. Then we will get ourselves in better perspective.

Getting Outside Ourselves

In order to understand the challenge ahead, as much as we need to do some self-analysis in regard to generational tendencies, we need even more to cultivate an outward rather than an inward focus. The whole thrust of the world around us would be to turn us inward, even in order to find God. Many of the early years of the new millennium were marked (in the United States but also internationally) by best-seller self-help books that included statements like this: "You are God in a physical body. You are Spirit in the flesh. You are Eternal Life expressing itself as You. You are a cosmic being. You are all power. You are all wisdom. You are all intelligence. You are perfection. You are magnificence. You are the creator, and you are creating the creation of You on this planet."[2]

Sue Monk Kidd, a popular author especially among women, resonates with this inward focus. In her spiritual autobiography, a book full of references to Scripture as well as to many self-help books, she tells extensively about that process of finding the "True Self" within, the "inner Divine, the God-image, the truest part of us":

> The important thing became not saving the soul but entering it, greening it, developing the divine seed that waits realization. . . . It was as if God were whispering to me, The soul wants to be acknowledged and nurtured. The True Self wants to bloom and grow. And the way to begin this spiritual flowering is to confront your false selves—the ego patterns you have created—and come home to who you really are inside.[3]

Kidd is clearly on to something, but she consistently ends up inside herself to find it—as do the main characters in her widely read novels. Such voices are the popular versions of the voices in scholarly circles or even in the church that tell readers in general and readers of the Bible that their role is to decide for themselves what a text means, according to their own contexts and experiences, without studying to know the authors and ultimately the Author. When Kidd explains her "grounding," along with the Bible she mentions centuries of Christian spiritual writing, developmental psychology, and "*contemporary spiritual direction*" (my emphasis).[4] The contemporary spiritual direction is increasingly clear, and it is inward. This inside-out approach does not simply constitute an epistemological or metaphysical or hermeneutical problem; it has permeated our culture.

Such an inward focus works against Bible study as we have been discussing it. I do not mean to say that our inner experience is not hugely important or that we should ignore it. I *do* mean to say that the reading and studying of Scripture should be like a wind blowing from outside us into us, rather than from inside us onto a page of dancing words that our own breath settles. The first truth we discussed, the fact that Scripture is God speaking, or God-breathed, establishes this direction. We can either open ourselves to it, by the power of the Spirit, or close ourselves to it and turn inward, finally listening only to our own voice.

The prophet Isaiah brings God's word to warn us of the folly of mistaking our voice for his:

> For my thoughts are not your thoughts,
>   neither are your ways my ways, declares the LORD.
> For as the heavens are higher than the earth,
>   so are my ways higher than your ways
>   and my thoughts than your thoughts. (Isa. 55:8–9)

And then Isaiah gives us a picture to make it vivid:

> For as the rain and the snow come down from heaven
>   and do not return there but water the earth,
>   making it bring forth and sprout,
>   giving seed to the sower and bread to the eater,

153

> so shall my word be that goes out from my mouth;
> it shall not return to me empty,
> but it shall accomplish that which I purpose,
> and shall succeed in the thing for which I sent it.
> (Isa. 55:10–11)

The picture is of a transcendent word, coming from outside of us and above us, from a sovereign, personal heavenly provider—one who is actually providing these words and speaking these words about his provision at the same time. The seed is not within us to find; the seed is sent us from heaven.

Isaiah's lines picture well the truths we have discussed in this book. The Bible is *God speaking*: in these God-breathed words God tells us his word goes out from his mouth. The Bible is *powerful*: this word will not return void, without accomplishing everything God intends. The Bible is *understandable*: it is not sent out into a void but sent for a purpose that is like the purpose of giving seed to the sower and bread to the eater. These pictures connect the word with people who receive it. They reverberate throughout all of Scripture, reminding us of the parable of the sower, of God saying that man shall not live by bread alone, and of Jesus telling us that he is the bread of life. These are pictures of God's purpose to connect his word personally with those who receive and understand it. The Bible is a *literary work*: here we have one of the most beautiful examples of its imagery, so that in the process of these poetic lines we are taking in God's Word and the truth of God's Word not just through propositions but in fact imaginatively, through pictures of concrete things like rain and snow and seed and bread.

Finally, these lines from Isaiah 55 point to the fact that God's Word is *one whole story*. We already related these pictures to other parts of the Bible, and they already led us to Jesus and the parable of the seed and Jesus the bread of life. This picture is the highest-up metanarrative, telling of a sovereign God sending his word from heaven according to his perfect purpose, which will be accomplished without fail. It is perhaps too much of a stretch to make the direct connection and call this passage a picture of God's sending his Son, Jesus the Word made flesh, to accomplish the salvation purposed from the beginning, before returning to heaven. It is not too much of a stretch, however, to consider all the words of Scripture as God's proclamation from heaven of his purpose to save, ultimately through his Son. This is the big story of the universe revealed to us in Scripture from beginning to end.

It is a story bigger than any of our individual stories; it is outside all of them and holds them all together. The wonder is that a voice from outside breaks in and tells us the story. We could never get it on our own because our thoughts are not God's thoughts and his ways are not ours. Because his are much higher, sometimes they seem utterly alien and extremely difficult. But what a mercy that he opens his thoughts and ways to us in his Word. The completely countercultural challenge is to lift up our eyes from ourselves and believe the big story as God tells it, in fact sends his Word into it, to accomplish his ultimate purpose of redemption for his people.

The Word's description of itself as God's voice coming to us from outside ourselves revolutionizes our perspective on it in every way. The point in the end becomes not so much that we look outside ourselves to find a set of truths to which we must give intellectual assent. The process is *personal*: we look up to hear someone's voice and find someone there. In the end, the point is that the true God speaks his true word to us, and we must receive it and receive him in the process.

> "At the end of each semester we have a meal together to celebrate what God has done through his Word. I'm continually amazed at how God has been at work, quietly transforming hearts and lives. Just last spring we heard from several women who had come to have a personal relationship with Jesus as we studied 1 and 2 Thessalonians and 1 and 2 Kings. These are not generally books that one would use for evangelism, but as we all heard their stories, we were reminded that the Lord uses all of his Word to accomplish his purposes. These personal testimonies provide evidence that the Bible is not simply a book of good moral teaching. It truly is 'living and active'!"
>
> —Cindy Cochrum, Bible study teacher,
> College Church in Wheaton, Illinois

Nothing New

Part of the result of getting outside ourselves will be a renewed look inward, but with the right perspective—with repentance and humility. The challenges we have discussed are not only culturally based; they are universal because they originate in sinful hearts. Our sinful hearts prejudge others, treat others selfishly, and refuse to look up and acknowledge that God is God and I am not.

Kevin Vanhoozer identifies two "interpretive sins," pride and sloth, which he helpfully connects directly with the process of reading and studying Scripture. Pride, he says, can make us think we easily "master" the meaning of a text without submitting ourselves to the work of studying it. Or pride can refuse to acknowledge that meaning is possible, thus effectively repudiating the author and his intent.[5] Vanhoozer's discussion of sloth is fascinating and convicting:

> Those on the theological right are slothful when, instead of interpreting for themselves, they rely on someone else—the Spirit, a television preacher, a teacher—to tell them what the text means. Those on the theological left are similarly slothful when, instead of working towards the best interpretation, they remain satisfied with a plethora of conflicting, often contradictory, readings. Interpretive sloth thus ignores the voice of the other every bit as much as does interpretive pride.[6]

R. C. Sproul gets at the same problem of sloth in a more blunt way, plainly calling Bible study "work" and then offering his verdict: "Our problem is not a lack of intelligence or a lack of passion. Our problem is that we are lazy."[7]

"Lecture only, with no homework or preparation, is very non-threatening for the new person and is a good way to lay down the basics of the faith. But there is only so much growth that occurs with spoon-feeding. Eventually, to mature, the student must learn to chew on deeper things in God's Word by grappling with them for himself or herself."

—Mary Beth McGreevy, Visiting Instructor, Covenant Theological Seminary, St. Louis, Missouri

---

Sloth . . . pride . . . selfishness . . . rebellion against God . . . clearly, it is our own sinful hearts that often keep us from receiving the Word of God as we should. These are not new challenges; they are as old as the fall, which began with a willful mishandling of God's clear word. Even though generational tensions may develop new wrinkles, they are not new, nor are they the root of the problem, which is as old as the first generation. That call to turn our attention inward instead of outward does seem to permeate the culture more blatantly than ever before, but it is in the end just another manifestation of the idolatrous desire to worship self rather than to worship God.

"I believe we should emphasize the place of prayer in every aspect of Bible study. In preparation, reading, observing, and application, we will be lacking without prayer."

—JoAnn Cairns, Bible study author and teacher,
College Church in Wheaton, Illinois

The Bible itself tells of a holy God and lets us see our sinful selves in light of him. It also lets us see the way of redemption from our sin through the Lord Jesus Christ. The only solutions to the problems we have with studying the Word are found in the Word. The only final solution is indeed not in ourselves but in the God who calls us to hear his voice and enables us to do so. Prayerfully, humbly, repentantly, through Christ, by the power of the Spirit, we can become the ground where the seed sprouts and grows and bears fruit.

Conclusion

Looking Ahead . . .

The Promise

The promise:

1. Nothing (but everything) new
2. The end of the story
3. Fruit

LOOKING INTO THE FUTURE OF BIBLE STUDY, we should see great challenge but even greater promise. I will conclude by speaking briefly of the promise of the future. It is what we have been talking about all along: it is the promise given us in the Word itself.

Nothing (But Everything) New

Just as we concluded that the challenge of Bible study is actually nothing new, so we must similarly conclude with the promise. It is the Word itself that puts before us all those seeds sprouting and trees growing and deserts blooming and fruit appearing—from Genesis all the way to Revelation. Those pictures communicate the promise of taking in the Word: life through the written Word sown on good soil, and life through the living Word who enters and transforms a heart.

In the end, we can put our hope not in our good methods (which we do need), not in some dramatic new development (which might occur), but in the very old promises of God that are always new, generation after generation. In this book I point to words written down a long time ago so that God's people from one generation to the next could know the redemptive story and join in its flow. The words are old, but the ongoing life is always new.

We by nature tend to want new things; newness makes us feel that there is promise, progress, and hope. That's why retailers can keep us shopping—because we love and long for new things. Studying this oldest of books lets us hear the voice of the one who says, "I am making all things new" (Rev. 21:5). The gospel is a story of new clothes and new hearts. Newness brought about by God is as old as the universe itself. It just keeps happening, and it will keep happening according to the purpose of the God who spoke the words—until Jesus comes again and the story is complete.

The End of the Story

The story is indeed heading somewhere, as we've seen not only in Paul's letter to the Thessalonians but also in the whole big story of Scripture breathed out by God from beginning to end. We have noted that its patterns and types are not repetitive or cyclical; they develop and unfold as they build up to the climax, centered in the person of Jesus. The promise of studying the Bible is finding life in Jesus not just *now* through faith, but *forever*, during eternity that will begin when Jesus comes to earth again and all things will finally be made new.

To study such a story is to jump onto a moving train and feel the powerful momentum of God's promises forging ahead toward the redemption of a people from all the nations of the world, forever. The destination is revealed by John in that final picture of God's people together with him in a new heaven and earth. Jesus clearly told his disciples that he was going away to prepare a place for them and that he was coming back to judge the world and to gather his people in that place. It has to end there!

In the meantime in which we live, in motion toward the end, God has given this Word not just to guide and comfort his people but also to accomplish that urgent gospel work of drawing people to himself, making them "wise for salvation through faith in Christ Jesus" (2 Tim. 3:15). Through the guidance of preachers and teachers and parents and mentors and all kinds of Word-lovers, this Word will in these last days continue to draw people to Christ, until the last day when every eye will see him either as Savior or as Judge. The whole story of salvation gives us needed perspective on the urgency of studying and training others to study the Word, with the end in view.

I love to picture that moment when Jesus called his disciples to lift up their eyes and see that "the fields are white for harvest," ready to yield up "fruit for eternal life" (John 4:35–36). That powerful little teaching moment inserts itself in John's narrative between the story of the Samaritan woman believing and the continuation of the story in which many people from her town believe as well. The metaphorical teaching is embedded at the heart of a story of the harvest actually happening, as that Samaritan town yields up its fruit—not just

161

one, but many. The sower is Jesus and secondarily an unlikely Samaritan, the one who has just heard the news herself.

What we have here is a picture of the gospel reaching the world and taking off. The woman's testimony draws the people to meet and hear Jesus for themselves: "And many more believed because of his word. They said to the woman, 'It is no longer because of what you said that we believe, for we have heard for ourselves, and we know that this is indeed the Savior of the world'" (John 4:41–42).

"My observation is that most non-churchgoers are vaguely familiar with a few stories from the Bible, most likely from their childhood. Often there is a precipitating event in their adult lives that piques their curiosity about the Bible. They know that other people have found faith and solace in its pages. Would it make a difference in their lives? Three of the women who have attended Bible study with me had all gone through some recent hardship: battling cancer, a surprise pregnancy that almost ended in abortion, the death of a mother and sister within months of each other. All were searching for answers, for meaning, to make some sense out of the circumstances of their lives. They thought there might be something in the Bible for them, and they were willing to give it a chance."

—Deb Lorentsen, Curriculum Coordinator for Women's Bible Study, College Church in Wheaton, Illinois

---

Jesus the Savior of the world is coming back to this earth. We are headed full steam toward that moment, powered on our way by the promises of God. Until we see Jesus face-to-face, we his people have a chance to lift up our eyes and see the work that can be done, the harvest of life that can be sown and reaped, through the Word.

Fruit

Until that day we have the work of sowing and reaping, but in the process we can also enjoy the growing fruit. The fruit of studying the Bible has been scattered regularly throughout this discussion. Let's end by gathering it up and relishing the feast given through the Word. I will not be comprehensive in summing up the fruit of Bible study; the fruit is abundant, interconnected, and ever-growing.

First and foremost, as we have stressed, the fruit of studying the Word is *new life in Christ*: through his Word, by his Spirit, God draws people to come to know him through faith in his Son. This happens when unbelievers study the Word directly, especially among believers who can show the way. It happens also when believers who are studying can effectively share with unbelievers the fruit of their study—starting in the home and moving outward into all the settings of life.

We all know the amazing way God can take a passage we're studying and weave it into our ongoing conversations and relationships. If we're full of it, it will out! We all know as well the way evil from our hearts can well up into our words. "Out of the abundance of the heart the mouth speaks," Jesus said (Matt. 12:34). The great British preacher Charles Spurgeon in one of his sermons referred to the writer John Bunyan: "Prick him anywhere—his blood is Bibline—the very essence of the Bible flows from him! He cannot speak without quoting a text, for his very soul is full of the Word of God. I commend his example to you."[1]

Such an example points as well to the fruit of *sanctification* in a believer's life—not an impersonal process of performing better and better works, but a personal process of knowing God better and better and so desiring to please him and to be conformed to the image of his Son. Scripture's many images of the Word as the sword (Eph. 6:17 and Heb. 4:12, for example) communicate the power of the Word, by the Spirit, to pierce hearts with conviction of sin and knowledge of a holy God— not only for the first time, but persistently, and increasingly. The kind of Bible study that digs humbly and deeply into God's Word to hear him speaking will allow that Word a most effective route into the heart and mind, as the Spirit takes our work and does his work.

"Every year I have been a part of our Bible study, I have seen God use his Word to transform hearts and lives. We have had women from nearly every background, every denomination, every educational level, and every social standing arrive on the first day of Bible study with no grasp of who Jesus is or how to approach God's Word. Then at year's end, many stand and tell of how they have come to have a personal relationship with God through the study of his Word. They have often gone home and shared the gospel with family members, who have also come to know Jesus through their witness. The study of God's Word will change lives. God promises to use his Word. We have found that to be true, year after year."

—Cindy Cochrum, Bible study teacher, College Church in Wheaton, Illinois

The picture of a sword connects to scenes of battle and reminds us that we have no power of ourselves in what is indeed a battle against evil; only through the Word of the one who has won the battle can we fight effectively. When Paul tells Timothy that all Scripture is God-breathed, he in the same breath goes on to describe its power to shape a person in godliness: it is "profitable for teaching, for reproof, for correction, and for training in righteousness, that the man of God may be competent, equipped for every good work" (2 Tim. 3:16–17). The pile-up of profits that Paul lists here does not portray an easy or a gentle process; rather, Paul sends forth almost a battering ram of strong, tough sorts of words to portray the kind of battle that requires such a powerful sword in order to win. The psalmist is not asking a theoretical question when he asks, "How can a young man keep his way pure?" The answer again comes in battle terminology: "By guarding it according to your word" (Ps. 119:9).

Paul's example evidences the way this battle brings suffering—suffering often brought about through a faithful witness to the gospel, and suffering that results from living in this broken world. But all of it is suffering planned by a sovereign God whose consistent intention is to glorify his Son and to make his people more like him. We know that "all things work together for good, for those who are called according to his purpose." We read on and find that purpose: "For those whom he foreknew he also predestined to be conformed to the image of his Son" (Rom. 8:28–29). The suffering involved in this process of sanctification leads to another wonderful fruit of studying the Word: *comfort in the midst of suffering.*

In the midst of grief countless followers of God have fed on words like those from Psalm 77 and Psalms 42–43 and thereby found a way to look up to the God of comfort. Paul wrote inspired words of comfort that have for generations turned people to the gospel comfort they have received and that flows from them to others (2 Cor. 1:3–7). We have all probably witnessed the way God brings verses and passages that have been studied back to the minds and hearts of those in desperate need. How much better to face troubles with that Word in us and already at work than to "go digging" when the troubles come.

The ultimate comfort we find in Scripture is the very comfort of Christ himself, who came to provide "eternal comfort" (2 Thess. 2:16–17) through his death and resurrection. The eternal comfort is the comfort of eternity with him. In the meantime, as we trust and hope, Scripture might be regarded as the ultimate healthy "comfort food," the manna from heaven that is sweet like honey and satisfies our souls even in the midst of the most severe hardship.

The fruit of *guidance in the midst of perplexity* is a fruit perhaps related to that of comfort, as the Word helps us needy and limited human beings along our way. Perhaps this is one of the more misunderstood fruits, as we tend to search the Scriptures intently when we face life-changing decisions concerning career, marriage, changing location, etc. Of course, general principles can be found—such as that marriage is indeed a good thing (Prov. 18:22; Heb. 13:4)! However, a person might better understand Scripture's teaching on marriage in the context of the whole story, from Genesis through Song of Solomon through the New Testament all the way to the picture of the marriage feast in Revelation.

The point is that it is generally less profitable to search the Bible for a specific spurt of guidance about a concrete action than to study the Bible in a deep, ongoing way so that its wisdom will shape and inform every concrete decision

166

of our life. It is more fundamental to be guided into conformity with the image of Christ than to be guided into just the right career move. In fact, such guidance is connected, as the fruit of sanctification leads to the fruit of guidance in perplexity.

"Some time ago, our family faced a ministry opportunity that was unexpected and unconventional, and that required a large step of faith on my part. The previous year our women's Bible study had been working in the book of James. The Lord used that study to prepare me to be willing to follow God's leading in spite of my fears and weaknesses. Was it a particular verse or section of Scripture that spoke to me? Not really. Rather, it was the weekly vision of who God is and his call to walk humbly with him. God was asking me to do kingdom work, to risk and to rest. So often we pray for guidance and direction, wondering about God's will for our lives. Well, this call was unmistakable. I can honestly say that without the foundation of God's Word through that Bible study, I may not have been ready to follow the Lord's leading. But by God's grace he had already given me all I needed to obey."

—Lisa Helm, Bible study leader and pastor's wife,
Holy Trinity Church, Chicago, Illinois

Perhaps the most fruitful guidance comes when we study the Word with others in the body of Christ. The fruit of *fellowship in the Word* is one of the sweetest fruits, as food shared is most enjoyed. We were made to hear God's voice both individually and as his called-out people. The apostle Paul often exhorts the church community to this kind of fellowship, as in the case of the Colossians: "Let the word of Christ dwell in you richly, teaching and admonishing one another in all wisdom, singing psalms and hymns and spiritual songs, with thankfulness in your hearts to God" (Col. 3:16). The role of preaching stands central in this communal taking in of the Word, as it is proclaimed with authority to the gathered church. Supplementing that preaching should be a whole swarm of teachers and studiers of the Word, so that its living and active power is known and shared throughout the body. I could never sum up or measure the encouragement and wisdom I've received from those with whom I have studied the Bible over the years.

"God has allowed me to use my experience and training in a volunteer teaching role for the women of Lookout Mountain Presbyterian Church. It has been my deep joy to see God's Word become alive in many people. . . . We have found that a weekly commitment to studying the Word of God spurs the group on to be diligent in study together. Dividing into groups of five to fifteen allows for more individual participation and application. The discussion time combined with a time of prayer and sharing deepens our fellowship. All these things, along with the developing friendships, give rise to practical actions of service that can be a witness to Christ's love to others in the community."

—Wendy Williams, Bible study leader, Lookout Mountain
Presbyterian Church, Lookout Mountain, Tennessee

Finally, and perhaps especially in the fellowship of God's people, all this sowing and reaping brings the fruit of *joy*. In that teaching interlude we observed in John 4, Jesus puts it this way: "Already the one who reaps is receiving wages and gathering fruit for eternal life, so that the sower and reaper may rejoice together" (John 4:36). The very process of the Word doing its work brings joy. Philip's newly baptized eunuch friend went on his way rejoicing (Acts 8:39). That scene from Nehemiah, with God's people gathered, ends: "And all the people went their way to eat and drink and to send portions and to make great rejoicing, because they had understood the words that were declared to them" (Neh. 8:12).

Scripture overflows with witness to the joy of taking in God's words deeply and believingly. Psalm 119 offers one long praise/prayer about the Word: "How sweet are your words to my taste," the psalmist cries, "sweeter than honey to my mouth!" (Ps. 119:103). Many other passages express not only this delight but also this vivid, concrete picture of eating the Word and finding it sweet. David writes: "The precepts of the LORD are right, rejoicing the heart." In the same passage he calls God's words "sweeter also than honey and drippings of the honeycomb" (Ps. 19:8, 10). The parallel lines in these psalms reveal the joy to be not a separate feeling but actually connected to the righteousness and perfection of a Law that reveals the righteousness and perfection of God himself. Jeremiah speaks to God of "your words" that "became . . . joy":

> Your words were found, and I ate them,
>   and your words became to me a joy
>   and the delight of my heart. (Jer. 15:16)

What does this picture of eating communicate? Actively taking in . . . chewing . . . tasting . . . digesting . . . communal enjoyment . . . the satisfaction of satiated hunger . . . getting hungry again and again . . . The many aspects of this metaphor call us not only to deep personal meditation and reflection but also to the work of study. Studying the Scriptures and increasingly understanding them makes it possible to get their real taste and to digest them deeply. Studying the Scriptures, however, is not just the hard part that results in joy. The process of study increasingly becomes a joyful activity in itself, as we learn and teach the truth of God that feeds our souls. Many a student of God's Word knows the delight of discovery that invades the process of working to understand a text. It's not ultimately solving some textual riddle; it's the joyful experience of hearing God's voice even more clearly and reveling in the breath of his very presence.

"My prayer for friends, and for those who do not yet have the confidence of salvation that comes through Christ, is that they would be *really hungry and thirsty for God's Word, themselves.* When this happens, there will be no stopping them."

—Deb Lorentsen, Curriculum Coordinator for Women's Bible Study, College Church in Wheaton, Illinois

---

We would do well to read the Puritans on the study of the Word. They reveled in all the metaphors of God's Word as our piercing sword of conviction of sin, our armor for battle, our comforting and healing medicine in sorrow, and our guide to putting on the clothes of righteousness. But their eloquence concerning the deep delight of taking in the Word should strike us with special challenge and conviction. Do we know this delight? Do we value the Word in this way? Thomas Watson, Puritan preacher and writer of seventeenth-century Britain, writes:

> When you read the word, look on it as a soul-enriching treasury. Search here as for a vein of silver (Prov. 2:4). In this word are scattered many divine aphorisms; gather them up as so many jewels. This blessed book helps to enrich you; it fills your head with knowledge and your heart with grace. It stores you with promises. A man may be rich in bonds. In this field the pearl of price is hidden. What are all the world's riches compared to these? Islands of spices, coasts of pearl, rocks of diamonds—these are but the riches that reprobates may have, but the word gives us those riches which angels have.[2]

We saw that picture from Isaiah 55, in which God's word like the rain and the snow coming down from heaven accomplishes without fail his purpose. That picture is followed immediately in the text by another picture, one that goes on to portray the joy of God's word coming to pass, ultimately in Jesus. This next picture shows the bursting forth of all the trees and growing things we have seen as the promise of the Word. It is a picture that joyfully reaches for the Savior who came and who is coming again. May we who study the Scriptures know this joy, in and through Christ the living Word.

> For you shall go out in joy
>   and be led forth in peace;

171

the mountains and the hills before you
    shall break forth into singing,
    and all the trees of the field shall clap their hands.
Instead of the thorn shall come up the cypress;
    instead of the brier shall come up the myrtle;
and it shall make a name for the LORD,
    an everlasting sign that shall not be cut off.
       (Isa. 55:12–13)

Appendix

Genre-Specific Study Questions

by David Helm, Executive Director of the Charles Simeon Trust

THESE QUESTIONS ARE PART OF A FORTHCOMING BOOKLET, tentatively titled *One-to-One*, to be published by Matthias Media. They are used with permission of David Helm and Matthias Media.

Study Questions for the Gospels and Acts

1. How does the author describe the plot in terms of characters, conflict, climax, and resolution? What is the author's emphasis?

2. How might the passages on either side of this text inform our understanding of the text?

3. What surprises, if any, are in the story? Does anyone answer, speak, or behave in an unexpected way?

4. In what ways does the text contribute to our understanding of the death and resurrection of Jesus?

5. How do you think *this* text might serve the author's overall objective in writing?

6. How do the characters in this narrative respond to Jesus' authority, death, or resurrection? What does their response teach us about our own?

7. How does the author intend this text to affect our lives individually and/or corporately?

Study Questions for Old Testament Narrative

1. How does the author describe the main characters, and how do they describe each other? How do these characters function in the story?

2. What are the conflict (or climax) and resolution in the text? What is the author's emphasis?

3. What surprises, if any, are in the story? Does anyone behave in an unexpected way?

4. Sometimes Old Testament narrative doesn't directly address the gospel, but it might connect to the gospel by some other means (such as example, irony, or antithesis). How does this text anticipate the gospel?

5. How is the gospel the answer to the issues and questions raised by this text?

6. What is the main point that the main characters are supposed to be learning in light of the gospel?

7. How might this main point be relevant to our lives?

Study Questions for the Epistles

1. What is the situation in the church or among the people to whom the letter is written? How does the text reveal that situation?

2. What argument is the author making, and how does the language and structure of the text support it?

3. What surprising or unexpected statements, if any, does the author make? How do these statements fit into the argument?

4. How does this text relate to other parts of this book?

5. How does the author reference Jesus Christ? If there is no explicit reference to Jesus Christ, how do the propositions and supporting points relate to the gospel?

6. What kind of change is the author trying to persuade his readers to make in their lives?

7. How might such a change be relevant for us in our day?

Study Questions for Hebrew Wisdom Literature/Poetry

1. Are there parallel phrases or similar ideas within the text, and what do these repetitions indicate about its structure and emphasis?

2. What images and metaphors are used by the author? What do they indicate about God or the people in the text?

3. How is this text, if at all, related to circumstances of the author's or other characters' lives as they are described in the historical (or Old Testament narrative) books?

4. How is this text related to the gospel of Jesus Christ? Are the life, death, and resurrection of Jesus anticipated in any way? Is this text referenced in the New Testament? If so, what is its significance?

5. What do we learn about God from this text? About ourselves?

6. What emotions is the author evoking, and what point is he trying to make by them?

7. Are there specific instructions/imperatives in the text? What consequences are there for us if we reject God's commands in this text?

Study Questions for Prophetic Literature

1. By paying attention to what the prophet says, what do we learn about God's plans?

2. How is this text related to the historical circumstances of Israel as described in other historical books of the Bible?

3. Look at the imagery used. How is the author alluding to other parts of the Old Testament in the text?

4. How is this text related to the gospel? Is Jesus anticipated in any way?

5. How do the words of the prophet convict God's people for their failure to keep God's Word?

6. How do the words of the prophet comfort God's people that God's gracious promises to them will still be kept?

7. What kinds of responses (ethical and otherwise) are demanded from those hearing the words of this prophet? How ought we to respond, both individually and corporately?

Study Questions for Apocalyptic Literature

1. What is the situation or what are the conditions among the people to whom the apocalypse is written? How does the text reveal that situation?

2. What images and symbols are used in this text? What effect do they have on you as reader?

3. Where do these symbols appear elsewhere in the Bible? And what, if any, connection does the author intend for us to make?

4. What in the text demonstrates that we are reading about events from God's vantage point of history? What comfort and insight does this provide for our human perspective of history?

5. How does this text anticipate or recall the death, resurrection, and reign of Jesus Christ?

6. What is the tension or conflict in the text, and how does it relate both to the original readers and to us?

7. How does the text compel us to respond to the death, resurrection, and reign of Jesus Christ?

Notes

Introduction: What's Happening?

1. John Piper, "Brokers of the Book: Lessons from Luther for Pastors Today," *Journal of Beeson Divinity School* (Fall 2006): 5.

2. Lewis Carroll, *Through the Looking Glass* (New York: W. W. Norton, 1971), 163. I introduce one of my longtime favorite authorities on this subject, Humpty Dumpty, with a mixture of regret and delight at his increasing popularity as a voice in the discussion.

3. Kevin Vanhoozer, *Is There a Meaning in This Text? The Bible, the Reader, and the Morality of Literary Knowledge* (Grand Rapids: Zondervan, 1998). See chapter 2, "Undoing the Author: Authority and Intentionality," especially pp. 69–74.

4. Vern Sheridan Poythress, *In the Beginning Was the Word: Language— A God-Centered Approach* (Wheaton, IL: Crossway, 2009).

Chapter 1: If the Bible Is God Speaking . . . Then How Should We Listen?

1. Vaughan Roberts, *God's Big Picture: Tracing the Storyline of the Bible* (Downers Grove, IL: InterVarsity Press, 2002), 13.

2. David Jackman, *I Believe in the Bible* (London: Hodder & Stoughton, 2000), xii.

3. Carl Henry, *God, Revelation, and Authority*, 6 vols. (Wheaton, IL: Crossway, 1999).

Chapter 2: If the Bible Is Powerful . . . Then How Should We Approach It?

1. R. C. Sproul, *Knowing Scripture* (Downers Grove, IL: InterVarsity Press, 1977), 14–15.

2. Information for this example comes from Gordon D. Fee and Mark L. Strauss, *How to Choose a Translation for All Its Worth* (Grand Rapids: Zondervan, 2007), 90.

3. Merrill F. Unger and William White, eds., *Vine's Complete Expository Dictionary of Old and New Testament Words* (Nashville: Thomas Nelson, 1996).

4. Leland Ryken, *The Word of God in English: Criteria for Excellence in Bible Translation* (Wheaton, IL: Crossway, 2002). See also his *Understanding English Bible Translation: The Case for an Essentially Literal Approach* (Wheaton, IL: Crossway, 2009).

5. Fee and Strauss, *How to Choose a Translation.*

6. David Jackman, *I Believe in the Bible* (London: Hodder & Stoughton, 2000), 72.

7. Henry H. Halley, *Pocket Bible Handbook: An Abbreviated Bible Commentary* (Chicago: Henry H. Halley, 1948), 5.

Chapter 3: If the Bible Is Understandable . . . Then How Should We Get It?

1. John Dillenberger, ed., *Martin Luther: Selections from His Writings* (New York: Anchor Books, 1961), 172–73.

2. Timothy Larsen, "Literacy and Biblical Knowledge: The Victorian Age and Our Own," *Journal of the Evangelical Theological Society* 52, no. 3 (2009): 520.

3. This approach is used in the preaching and teaching workshops offered by the Charles Simeon Trust. Information can be found at its Web site: http://simeontrust.org/.

4. *ESV Study Bible* (Wheaton, IL: Crossway Bibles, 2008), 2275.

Chapter 4: Asking Questions . . . A Second Implication

1. The Simeon Trust, http://simeontrust.org.

2. David I. Smith, *Learning from the Stranger: Christian Faith and Cultural Diversity* (Grand Rapids: Eerdmans, 2009), 117–18.

Chapter 5: If the Bible Is a Literary Work . . . Then What Should We Expect?

1. Leland Ryken, *How to Read the Bible as Literature* (Grand Rapids: Zondervan, 1987), 11.

2. Leland Ryken, *Words of Delight: A Literary Introduction to the Bible* (Grand Rapids: Baker, 1987). See also his *Words of Life: A Literary Introduction to the New Testament* (Grand Rapids: Baker, 1987).

3. Leland Ryken, James C. Wilhoit, and Tremper Longman III, eds., *Dictionary of Biblical Imagery* (Downers Grove, IL: InterVarsity Press, 1998).

4. Robert Alter, *The World of Biblical Literature* (New York: HarperCollins, 1992), 25.

5. C. S. Lewis, *Reflections on the Psalms* (New York: Harcourt, Brace & World, 1958), 2–3.

6. Gordon D. Fee and Douglas Stuart, *How to Read the Bible for All Its Worth* (Grand Rapids: Zondervan, 2003).

7. Ryken, in his *Words of Delight* (120–25), treats well the domestic themes and setting of Ruth.

Chapter 6: From Prose to Poetry . . . More Literary Explorations

1. Derek Kidner, *The Wisdom of Proverbs, Job and Ecclesiastes: An Introduction to Wisdom Literature* (Downers Grove, IL: InterVarsity Press, 1985), 11.

Kidner introduces his book with the picture of a pilgrim stopping to "take a long look round."

2. C. S. Lewis, *Reflections on the Psalms* (New York: Harcourt, Brace & World, 1958), 4–5.

3. Kevin Vanhoozer, *Is There a Meaning in This Text? The Bible, the Reader, and the Morality of Literary Knowledge* (Grand Rapids: Zondervan, 1998), 312.

4. My understanding of Isaiah's shape is greatly influenced by Alec Motyer's *Isaiah: An Introduction and Commentary* (Downers Grove, IL: InterVarsity Press, 1999).

Chapter 7: If the Bible Is One Whole Story . . . Then How Should We Read It?

1. Graeme Goldsworthy, *Gospel and Kingdom: A Christian Interpretation of the Old Testament* (Carlisle, UK: Paternoster Press, 1994); Edmund P. Clowney, *The Unfolding Mystery: Discovering Christ in the Old Testament* (Phillipsburg, NJ: Presbyterian and Reformed, 1988); Vaughan Roberts, *God's Big Picture: Tracing the Storyline of the Bible* (Downers Grove, IL: InterVarsity Press, 2002). I was first and greatly influenced by Goldsworthy's *Gospel and Kingdom*, but it is worth noting that three of his volumes have now been published as *The Goldsworthy Trilogy: Gospel and Kingdom; Gospel and Wisdom; The Gospel in Revelation* (Carlisle, UK: Paternoster Press, 2000).

2. Mark Dever, *The Message of the Old Testament* (Wheaton, IL: Crossway, 2006), 35. The corresponding and correspondingly helpful volume *The Message of the New Testament* was published by Crossway in 2005.

3. Goldsworthy, *Gospel and Kingdom*, 69–71.

Chapter 8: Storyline Implications at Work

1. Derek Kidner, *The Proverbs: An Introduction and Commentary* (Downers Grove, IL: InterVarsity Press, 1964), 79.

2. Alec Motyer, *Isaiah: An Introduction and Commentary* (Downers Grove, IL: InterVarsity Press, 1999), 24.

Chapter 9: So . . . What Is Bible Study?

1. Colin Marshall and Tony Payne, *The Trellis and the Vine: The Ministry Mind-Shift That Changes Everything* (Kingsford, Australia: Matthias Media, 2009), 57.

2. Ibid., 90.

Chapter 10: Looking Ahead . . . The Challenge

1. *After* writing this whole section, I stopped to check my e-mail. In my box I found one of Al Mohler's regular blogs, this one titled " 'Like the Air They Breathe'—The Online Life of Kids." Mohler comments on a new report from the Kaiser Family Foundation citing 7½ hours a day (up

one hour in five years) as the average time spent by America's children in electronic media. By contrast, time spent reading books has declined. See http://www.albertmohler.com/2010/01/21/like-the-air-they-breathe -the-online-life-of-kids/.

2. Rhonda Byrne, *The Secret* (New York: Beyond Words Publishing, 2006), 164.

3. Sue Monk Kidd, *When the Heart Waits: Spiritual Direction for Life's Sacred Questions* (San Francisco: HarperCollins, 1992), 48–49.

4. Ibid., ix.

5. Kevin Vanhoozer, *Is There a Meaning in This Text? The Bible, the Reader, and the Morality of Literary Knowledge* (Grand Rapids: Zondervan, 1998), 462–63.

6. Ibid., 463.

7. R. C. Sproul, *Knowing Scripture* (Downers Grove, IL: InterVarsity Press, 1977), 17.

Conclusion: Looking Ahead . . . The Promise

1. Charles H. Spurgeon, "The Last Words of Christ on the Cross," Sermon no. 2644, Delivered at the Metropolitan Tabernacle, Newington, on Lord's-Day Evening, June 25, 1881: http://spurgeongems.org/vols43-45/chs2644 ./pdf (January 26, 2010).

2. Thomas Watson, *Heaven Taken by Storm: Showing the Holy Violence a Christian Is to Put Forth in the Pursuit after Glory* (Morgan, PA: Soli Deo Gloria Publications, 1997), 13.

A native of St. Louis, Missouri, **Kathleen Nielson** holds M.A. and Ph.D. degrees in literature from Vanderbilt University and a B.A. from Wheaton College (Illinois). She has taught in the English departments at Vanderbilt University, Bethel College (Minnesota), and Wheaton College. She is the author of numerous Bible studies, as well as various articles and poems. Kathleen has directed and taught women's Bible studies at several churches and speaks extensively at conferences and retreats. Kathleen is married to Dr. Niel Nielson, president of Covenant College in Lookout Mountain, Georgia. Kathleen and Niel have three sons and two beautiful daughters-in-law.